Sixty Miles to Be Baptized

The Life and Ministry of Elias Sias
Central Michigan Restoration Pioneer
1833–1911

DR. JAMES L. AMSTUTZ

WESTBOW
PRESS®
A DIVISION OF THOMAS NELSON
& ZONDERVAN

WestBow Press books may be ordered through booksellers or by contacting:

WestBow Press
A Division of Thomas Nelson & Zondervan
1663 Liberty Drive
Bloomington, IN 47403
www.westbowpress.com
1 (866) 928-1240

ISBN: 978-1-9736-5078-2 (sc)
ISBN: 978-1-9736-5079-9 (e)

Library of Congress Control Number: 2019902043

Print information available on the last page.

WestBow Press rev. date: 3/7/2019

About the Author

Jim Amstutz has been the Senior Minister of East Superior Christian Church in Alma, Michigan since 1998. He received his education from Great Lakes Christian College, B.R.E. (1987); Emmanuel School of Religion, M.Div. (1992); and Harding University Graduate School, D.Min. (2002). His passion for the Restoration Movement started early while growing up in north central Kentucky. Living an hour away from the Cane Ridge Meeting House Shrine in Paris, Kentucky, he made frequent trips to the shrine with his parents.

Serving in located ministry for over twenty five years, Dr. Amstutz has been dedicated to preaching and teaching the principles of the Restoration Movement in the congregations he has served. He has written articles for the <u>Restoration Quarterly</u> and the <u>Christian Standard</u> journals. In 2011 he wrote "100 Years of Faithful Service" a history of East Superior Christian Church.

Contents

Preface

In 2003 I heard the name Elias Sias for the first time at a local Minister's meeting. I was intrigued to know more about the man who was responsible for starting many Restoration churches in central Michigan. As I began my search for anything written about him, I was frustrated at the lack of information available. I then became determined to find as much information that I could about Mr. Sias and publish my findings.

After several years of research, I am confident that I have read all primary sources and secondary sources written. I have received copies of several local church histories and articles written in the Christian Standard.

It is the scope of this project to focus primarily on the personal dimension of Elias Sias. Mr. Sias was a prolific church planter in central Michigan. The details and exploits of the churches he started have been documented in Robert L. Girdwood's book The Stone-Campbell Movement In Michigan. I would refer you to this work for a list of the numerous churches Elias started. My intent is to expose the character of the man who devoted his life to the Restoration Movement in Michigan.

There were four primary sources consulted for my work. John T. Brown Churches of Christ; Robert L. Girdwood The Stone-Campbell Movement In Michigan; numerous articles in the Christian Standard; and church histories from the congregations that Elias started. In addition to these four sources there are several secondary sources available. From these sources I was able to piece together a picture of the personal life of Elias Sias.

The title is borrowed from a July 25, 1942 Christian Standard article written by Edwin Errett about the baptism of Elias. Permission to use the title was granted by Standard Publishing. Elias' picture on the cover was reprinted from Brown's book (pg. 250), public domain. It is not recorded when that picture was taken and is the only one known to have been taken of him.

Chapter one introduces you to the Sias family. It reveals how and why they came to the United States, where the family initially settled in the new land, and what brought Elias to central Michigan.

Chapter two explores Elias' conversion to Christianity and subsequent ordination into the Ministry. This chapter unveils the evangelistic zeal that drove Elias throughout his life. It will also show how he took an active part in community affairs before becoming a full-time evangelist.

Chapter three will take a brief look at Elias' evangelistic work in the state of Michigan. He took an active part in the development of the state Evangelistic Society and helped organize the districts of central Michigan. It is here where we get a glimpse of his abilities and what people thought of him.

Chapter four introduces the reader to Elias' key partners in ministry. Elisha Brooks and Randall Faurot worked along side of Elias for the first fifteen years of his ministry. Together they helped start the Restoration congregations in Gratiot County. Individually, Brooks and Faurot made their own unique contributions to the work of Christ.

Chapter five looks at the later years of his life. In this chapter we learn where he finally settled and died. We see how he felt about his life in retrospect and hear what other Restoration leaders of the day felt about him.

Chapter six serves as a conclusion. Here we make general observations and review the transcendent impact of Elias' life. This chapter offers practical suggestions to the discerning reader who would choose a similar calling.

As you read this book I hope you will appreciate the faith, determination, accomplishments and hardships experienced by this unsung giant of the Restoration Movement in Michigan.

Acknowledgments

Several individuals have been of great help and encouragement to me during the writing of this book. John Robinson, minister of Forest Hill Church of Christ, introduced me to Elias Sias and challenged me with the idea of writing a book about him. He has also been a valuable source of information about Elias and the early years of his ministry in Gratiot County.

Robert L. Girdwood, noted Restoration Movement historian in Michigan, provided me with multiple resources pertaining to Elias' evangelistic work in central Michigan and helpful advice. Russell Sias, descendant of Elias, emailed me PDF files from Azariah Boody Sias' books, which furnished invaluable family information.

Diane Jones-Dunham of Standard Publishing and John Mark Wade, Library Assistant at Emmanuel Christian Seminary, made PDF copies for me of every <u>Christian Standard</u> article that mentioned Elias Sias and Elisha Brooks. Their assistance to me in this area is invaluable.

Dr. Keith Wise, retired minister of St. Louis Church of Christ, who has been a friend and mentor to me offered a helpful critique of my work. Vicki Monroe and Annette Elder, also members of the St. Louis congregation and Sias family descendants who reviewed and enthusiastically approved the book.

Finally, my wife, Joyce, has sweetly supported me in this project just as she does all my endeavors. This book would not be possible apart from the help I have received from these individuals.

James L. Amstutz
Alma, Michigan
February 2016

CHAPTER I

Coming to America

America[1] was a newly discovered and uncharted continent in the sixteenth century. Spain, France and England were staking claims to the new land. Soon many Europeans would come to America seeking a new start in life. This proved to be true for the Sias family as well.

The Sias family came from France in the 1600's and eventually settled in the New England area.[2] Tradition says that originally three brothers (John Sr., Lawrence, and Solomon or Clement) came from France to the American Colonies in 1677 to escape religious persecution.[3] The Sias (Sieyes)[4] family belonged to the Huguenots[5] and were Protestants by faith. Very little is known and documented of the early years in

---

[1] The name "America" is first used in a geography book referring to the New World with Amerigo Vespucci getting credit for the discovery of the continent. http://faculty.washington.edu/qtaylor/a_us_history/0000_1600_timeline.htm. Internet. (Retrieved February 19, 2016).

[2] Azariah Boody Sias, Sias Family In America 1677 to 1952, vol. 1, (Florida: Florida Press, 1952), 7. See the map at the end of the chapter for the family origin. Map is courtesy of Onestopmap.com.

[3] The third brother was not specifically mentioned by name, however, based upon later information he possibly was named Solomon or Clement. Ibid., xxii.

[4] Sieyes was the French name but was changed to Sias in America for simplification and to avoid further persecution. Ibid.

[5] Huguenots were French Protestants inspired by the writings of John Calvin. They were persecuted by the Catholic church and eventually eliminated in France. "Huguenots" https://en.wikipedia.org/wiki/Huguenot. Internet.

America. The third unnamed brother was said to have gone to the West Indies, and no one knows what happened to Lawrence.[6]

The recording of Sias family history in America begins with the marriage of John Sias, Sr. and Ann Pitman at Wells, Maine in 1698.[7] After their marriage, John and Ann moved to Durham, New Hampshire to establish their home in 1699. They built their home on the Old Mast Road where they lived until their deaths.[8] The Siases produced eight children, all of whom settled close to the homestead and raised their large families. For the sake of expediency, from this point forward, I will focus upon the direct ancestral line of Elias.[9]

One hundred years quickly passed from the time John Sias and his brothers landed on the shores of America to the beginning of the Revolutionary War. It is improbable that John Sr. witnessed the beginning of the war but no doubt he would have been proud of his grandsons. Two of John Jr.'s sons participated in the Revolutionary War. Benjamin was a captain and led a group from Loudon, New Hampshire. Charles enlisted and served under his brother as a Revolutionary soldier.[10]

After the war, Charles moved his family to West Derby, Vermont and settled on a 640 acre farm.[11] Charles and Jane raised their ten children there and were eventually buried there. Like their predecessors, the Sias children settled close to their parents' home, with the exception of one. Solomon Sr. married Delinda Eveline Collingwood in 1789 and would move their family to Cattaraugus County, New York.[12]

Solomon and Delinda produced five children (Jane, Polly, John, Solomon Jr. and Sylvenus). Jane, Polly and John would raise their families and die in Vermont. Solomon Jr. and Sylvenus would eventually migrate to Michigan.[13]

---

[6] Sias, vol. 1, xxii.
[7] Ibid.
[8] Ibid., 3.
[9] See chart at the end of the chapter which outlines Elias' family tree.
[10] Ibid., xxiii.
[11] Ibid.
[12] Ibid., 61.
[13] Ibid.

The Move to Central Michigan

Central Michigan in the 1800's was nothing but a virgin forest and wild prairie.[14] The lumbering industry was the leading employer and attracted many from the east.[15] The Sias family were rugged men and came to central Michigan to labor in the lumber industry.[16] Azariah Sias writes, "the early Sias families established their homes, labored in the wilderness, faced all kinds of dangers, fought great forest fires and often lost the sight of their eyes; but they were strong men and women."[17]

Four years after Elias was born in 1833, his father moved their family from New York to Chatham, Ontario. Azariah says that Sylvenus did not come to Michigan until after his children were born. Sylvenus and Julia's last child (John B.) was born in 1840. Ten years later the Sias family moved to Ingham County Michigan.

Sylvenus purchased 160 acres in Gratiot County and began to develop it for their eventual relocation.[18] According to the Gratiot County historical records, Solomon Jr. came to Michigan four years after his brother Sylvenus.[19] He brought his family of seven up the Pine River from Saginaw by canoe. He purchased 20 acres on section 2, Pine River Township, and resided there.[20]

Sylvenus bought a parcel of land on the southwest quarter of section one of the Pine River Township. Isaac Errett, recalling his days in Muir, said that "immigrants began to pour into Gratiot County to obtain

---

[14] Willard D. Tucker, Gratiot County, Michigan, (Michigan: Seemann & Peters Press, 1913), 23.

[15] Bob Girdwood notes that the lumbering industry greatly contributed to growth of new churches in central Michigan. Robert L. Girdwood, The Restoration Movement In Michigan, (Michigan: N.P.: N.P., 1975), 4.

[16] Sias, 102.

[17] Ibid.

[18] The Forest Hill Church of Christ church history says that Sylvenus moved his family to the Pine River Township (Gratiot County)in 1854. John W. Robinson, A History of Forest Hill Church of Christ - 1859-1994, 2. The Sias family history did not record a date.

[19] Chapman Brothers, Portrait and Biographical Album of Gratiot County, (Michigan: Chapman Brothers, 1884), 349.

[20] Ibid.

lands at 50 cents an acre."[21] Sylvenus farmed and Julia was a doctor.[22] It is recorded that Julia "often walked many miles winter nights to administer to the sick or deliver a baby. One night she caught cold. Pneumonia and consumption followed, which took her life."[23]

In the Pine River Township history, Silas Moody says he came to Pine River April 29, 1861, from Medina County, Ohio. He mentions several individuals In the Pine River Township history, Silas Moody says he came to Pine River April 29, 1861, from Medina County, Ohio. He mentions several individuals as pioneers who were "here before me." Among the list of pioneers mentioned by Moody are Solomon and Sylvenus Sias.[24] Very little information is recorded about Solomon Jr. and his family. It is believed that he lived out his days and died at the home of his daughter, Ann Woodmansee, February 4, 1884.[25]

Elias Sias was the oldest child of four born to Sylvenus and Julia. He was sixteen when his family moved from Ontario to Michigan. As he

---

[21] Isaac Errett, "Michigan," Christian Standard, August 28, 1879. See Gratiot County map at the end of the chapter.
[22] Sylvenus & Julia's pictures were reprinted from the Sias family history. Sias, 74–75. Used with permission.
[23] Chapman Brothers, 73.
[24] Tucker, 481.
[25] Chapman Brothers, 349.

worked with his father building their new home, he would meet and eventually marry Amanda Clymer in 1855. Elias was twenty-one and Amanda was eighteen at the time of their marriage.[26]

Elias and Amanda made their home in St. Louis, Michigan and produced ten children.[27] In addition to his ministry endeavors, Elias farmed to support his family. Farming in Gratiot County was extremely difficult in pioneer days. The lowlands of Gratiot County were "undrained and malaria infested."[28] Donald Monroe, who was the secretary of the Michigan Christian Missionary Society around 1900, said that "Elias was a hard working pioneer farmer who knew the hardships of the early settlements in Michigan."[29] Elias and Amanda lived in their St. Louis home until 1873 when they moved to Bloomingdale.[30]

---

[26] Amanda was a descendant of George Clymer, a signer of the Declaration of Independence. Sias, 112.

[27] Elias & Amanda's pictures were reprinted from the Sias family history. Sias, 113–114. Used with permission.

[28] Robinson, 2.

[29] John T. Brown, <u>Churches of Christ</u>, (Louisville: John P. Morton and Company, 1904), 250.

[30] Elias & Amanda's log home picture was reprinted from the back of a postcard provided by the Disciples of Christ Historical Society. The source of the postcard is not known. Copyright (C)Christian Standard Media. Used by permission.

Community Participant

Like his predecessors, Elias was not content in being a passive member of his community. The Sias family history reveals that the Sias family impacted the communities they lived in positively. Elias was also an active participant in Gratiot County, and this was noted in two ways.

Freemasonry

It is not known when Elias joined the Masons but it is recorded that he was a charter member of the St. Louis Lodge No. 188, A.F. & A.M.[31] The first meeting of the Lodge was held on August 31, 1865. The St. Louis Lodge burned in 1887. They were unable to procure funds to rebuild from the Grand Lodge and were forced to close.[32] It is not clear the extent of Elias' involvement in the Freemasonry, however, it is evident he participated in facilitating its beginning in Gratiot County.

Public Office

On at least 2 occasions Elias ran for public office in Gratiot County. He ran for the position of Pine River Constable in 1857 and lost by 36 votes. In 1867 Elias ran for the public office of clerk in Seville Township. There were four individuals who ran for that office: Joseph Davis, Pat

---

[31] Chapman Brothers, 796. The initials A.F. & A.M. stand for Ancient Free & Accepted Masons. These are distinctive titles within the history of Freemasonry.
[32] Transactions of the Grand Lodge - Free and Accepted Masons of the State of Michigan, A.D. 1888–A.L. 5888, (Michigan: 1888), 78.

Eagan, David Hosford, and Elias Sias. Elias received 23 votes and lost by one vote to Joseph Davis.[33] It is not known (and probably doubtful) if Elias ever ran for public office of any kind again. Soon his life would change directions, and in retrospect, he would impact the lives of thousands through a new-found focus.

Conclusion

John Sias and his brothers came to an unsettled land to escape religious persecution in their homeland. Their descendants helped establish a new country and they built new communities everywhere they went. They were pioneers in life and faith.

Within a hundred years, the descendants of the Sias family would also help blaze a new trail on the religious frontier. Elias became a prominent religious leader in central Michigan. He devoted his life to the spreading of the Gospel, and thousands would be indebted to his labor.

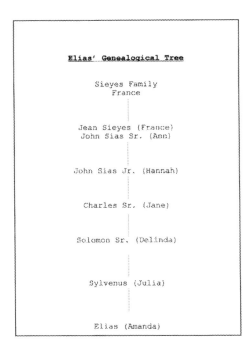

For an extensive list of the Sias family see Azariah Boody Sias' history.

---

[33] Tucker, 510.

MAP OF ORIGIN

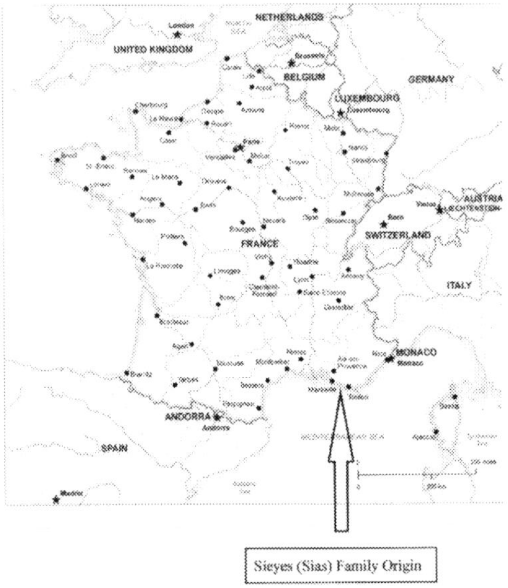

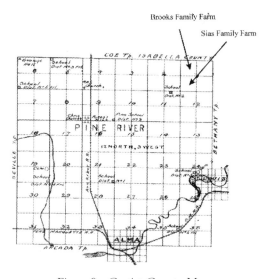

Sieyes (Sias) Family Origin

Figure 8

GRATIOT COUNTY MAP

Brooks Family Farm

Sias Family Farm

Figure 9 - Gratiot County Map

This map is from the early 1900's. The railroad did not come to Gratiot County until the late 1800's. The location of Sias' and Brooks' family farms is approximate based upon historical descriptions.

CHAPTER 2

Conversion to Christianity

The religious landscape of the nineteenth century in America was as diverse as the people who inhabited her. Europeans that came to America to experience religious freedom transplanted their religious diversity. While many denominational groups maintained their beliefs and traditions, some practices were altered in time.

One such practice that was changed was mankind's appropriation of salvation. For centuries, the church (regardless of denomination) was the vehicle through which salvation was offered. Through faith an individual responds to the offer and receives Christian baptism. This response then procures forgiveness of sins and church membership.

In spite of individual differences concerning the particularities of salvation, everyone agreed that salvation came through the church and culminated in Christian baptism. In the 1700's a subtle change began to take place in pulpits across America. Emotionalism was supplanting biblical truth and practice.

Eleazar Wheelock in 1741 adopted a new technique called the Mourner's Seat.[34] Using excessive emotion and fervor in his preaching, he would target sinners and call them forward to the front bench (pew) to receive salvation in prayer. According to eyewitnesses, false conversions were multiplied.

Within a hundred years the Mourner's Bench theology became a predominant practice in many churches. J. V. Coombs (a Disciples of

---

[34] See Appendix C for an explanation of how the Mourner's Seat developed into the popular Sinner's Prayer practice.

Christ minister, 1849) complained that the technique "drove many into a trance state."[35] Many revivalist preachers used the Mourner's Bench in place of Christian baptism. This was the theological landscape in Elias' day.

There are four accounts of Elias' conversion. One version states the event happened in 1857, the other three say it happened in 1858.[36] I am going to accept the 1857 date for two reasons: 1) the most extensive account of the event is recorded in a 1914 <u>Christian Standard</u> article, fifty-eight years after the event; 2) the Forest Hill Church of Christ history reports that their congregation began in the spring of 1859. It also says that Elias was baptized in the summer of 1858 and shortly thereafter was interested in starting a congregation in Forest Hill. Since there are no other discrepancies in the accounts of Elias' conversion other than the date, I will piece together what happened based upon the four accounts.It was the fall of 1857 and the Methodists held a camp-meeting near St. Louis. Elias and Amanda had been married for two years and lived in a clearing several miles from the meeting. The Siases attended the meeting and one evening decided to respond to the invitation. There at the Mourner's Bench they "made a start"[37]

A few months later in the spring of 1858, Elias met a neighbor, Elisha Brooks, who had moved from Indiana to Michigan. Mr. Brooks was a follower of the Restoration Movement and he gave to Elias a tract, "Sincerity Seeking the Way to Heaven."[38] The tract challenged the Mourner's Bench theology and other salvation beliefs of the day. It presented the simple New Testament plan of salvation.

Elisha studied the tract with Elias and Amanda for two weeks. Together they studied the tract along with the word of God. They then lent the tract to some neighbors and studied it with them. Soon there

---

[35] J. V. Coombs, Religious Delusions: A Psychic Study, (Cincinnati: Standard Publishing, 1904), 92.

[36] J. C. Meese, "The Restoration Movement in Central Michigan," Christian Standard, Vol. XLIX, No. 29, (July 18, 1914): 1237-1238, and Forest Hill Church of Christ history record an 1858 date. Edwin Errett, "Sixty Miles to Be Baptized," Christian Standard, Vol. CXXVII, No. 20, (July 25, 1942): 1-2, and John T. Brown's history of Churches of Christ give an 1858 date.

[37] Meese, 1237.

[38] I reproduced this tract in its entirety in Appendix A.

were eleven individuals who were ready to respond to the biblical plan of salvation. The group approached Elder Bartlett, a United Brethren preacher and asked him to baptize them; he refused.[39] According to the Bartlett family history, Elder Bartlett (Otis) was Elisha's father-in-law (see Appendix D). It is interesting that this connection is not noted in any of the historical reports of this event.

Not being able to find a minister to baptize them under the New Testament example, Elisha suggested that Elias go to Newville, Ind., the old home of Brooks, and be baptized by the Christian minister at that place, then return and baptize the others, or arrange for a minister to come and do it.[40]

Elias agreed to make the journey, but having no horse he decided to walk the 200 miles to Indiana. Elisha agreed to let Elias borrow a horse as soon as he had finished his work and could spare the animal. One morning while the Siases were eating breakfast, Elisha arrived with his horse. Elias prepared to go, said goodbye to his wife, and started for Indiana.

As Elias began his trip to Indiana he learned of a minister in Muir named Errett who preached the same things he had come to believe. He changed his course of direction and headed for Muir. When he arrived in Muir, he was told that Mr. Errett was accompanying Alexander Campbell on Missionary Society business.[41] It was arranged that an elder of the congregation, Ben Soule, would baptize Elias. After further discussion, it was also agreed that Mr. Soule and Darias Stone, another elder from the congregation, would come to Gratiot County in four weeks to baptize the others.[42] Elias was baptized in September of 1858 and returned home afterward.

---

[39] Brown, 250. It should be noted that at this time, the predominant mode of baptism was infant baptism or sprinkling for adults. Baptism by immersion for adults was an unheard of or new concept for many. This was one of the distinguishing factors of the Restoration Movement - it restored the biblical mode of baptism by immersion.

[40] It was the predominant practice at that time that an ordained minister or elder baptize and preside over the Lord's Supper. In the absence of a minister or elder another Christian could baptize. This belief would eventually change to any Christian can baptize.

[41] Edwin Errett, "Sixty Miles to Be Baptized," Christian Standard, Vol. CXXVII, No. 20, (July 25, 1942): 2.

[42] Brown, 250.

Ben Soule and Lumber Evangelism

The lumbering industry played a huge role in the early development of Michigan. During the middle 1800's the lumber trade contributed to the industrialization of Michigan through steamships and railroads.[43] It also helped advance the cause of the Restoration Movement.

Edwin Errett noted that "a group of business men, all members of the church of Christ, conceived the idea of organizing a lumber business, purchasing a tract of timber in the center of the state and taking into their business as a silent partner a Christian minister who would locate on their property and proceed to establish a church of Christ in this virgin territory."[44]

The minister they chose for this position was 35 year old Isaac Errett. Errett viewed this as a call from God. Against the advice of his friends, he turned down a lucrative offer from a church in Springfield, Ill. and moved his family into a log cabin 30 miles north of Lansing.[45]

The lumbering business failed and Isaac's family was plagued with illnesses. He continued to build a church in the local schoolhouse. The community would eventually be named Muir and the impact of Errett's determination upon the churches in mid Michigan would be huge.[46]

Ben Soule, known as "Uncle Ben,"[47] one of the partners of the lumber company, eventually became an elder of the Muir congregation. As previously noted, Uncle Ben baptized Elias Sias and would play a large role in the beginning of the first churches of Christ in central Michigan. All of this was the result of an entrepreneurial evangelistic spirit of a few businessmen.

---

[43] Robert L. Girdwood, The Stone-Campbell Movement In Michigan, (N.P.: N.P., 2001), 36.

[44] Errett, 2.

[45] Ibid.

[46] Gary L. Hawes, <u>The Life and Times of Isaac Errett</u>, Ph. D. Diss., (California: California Graduate School of Theology, 1984), 50.

[47] Ibid.

The Pine River Churches

The baptism of Elias Sias is marked as the beginning of the churches of Christ in the Pine River township. In 1856 a Bible School was started in the home of A. V. Packer.[48] The Bible School was eventually moved to the schoolhouse that had been erected at Curtis Corner (Forest Hill). Elias was not satisfied with simply a Bible School in the community. He wanted a church and he wanted to take an active part in that church.[49]

After baptizing Elias, Mr. Soule agreed to come to Gratiot County and baptize the others who were waiting.[50] Within four weeks Elder Soule arrived in St. Louis, and the remaining group of eleven were baptized. It is at this point where the historical records are in conflict with each other.

The Forest Hill church history says that Elias went from house to house announcing that Mr. Soule was coming and the gospel would be preached and a church would be started in the community. Settlers came together for a meeting which resulted in organizing a church of fourteen members in early 1859. Soule could not stay with the infant church and returned home to Muir.[51]

Meese writes that with "earnest solicitation" the young disciples encouraged Randal Faurot to come from Newville, Indiana. He agreed to come, baptized another candidate, and organized a church with twelve members.[52] Errett and Brown write that this was the beginning of two congregations, St. Louis and Forest Hill.[53] Bob Girdwood in his book The Stone-Campbell Movement In Michigan says that "the single

---

[48] Robinson, 2.

[49] Ibid.

[50] Here is another discrepancy in the stories. Meese says that Soule agreed to come to Michigan in two weeks, whereas Brown states that it was four weeks.

[51] Robinson, 2.

[52] Meese, 5.

[53] Brown, 250; Errett, 2. Errett indicates that a congregation was started at St. Louis in the country but later divided. One part moved into St. Louis (the town) and the other part started the congregation at Forest Hill.

congregation centered at Forest Hill made the decision to divide into three churches - Forest Hill, St. Louis, and Coe.[54]

So what can we conclude about the origin of Forest Hill, St. Louis, and Coe congregations? It is safe to assume that the nucleus of all three congregations came from the group of individuals that Ben Soule baptized in 1858. Whether we can say that this is a start date of a specific congregation is questionable. At best, we can say a congregation in the Pine River Township was started in 1858. From this congregation, two others were later formed, probably in 1859.

A Ministry Challenge

Before Ben Soule left Gratiot County, he challenged Elias Sias and Elisha Brooks to prepare themselves for the ministry of preaching and teaching the gospel.[55] It is not certain if Mr. Soule was simply planting a seed thought in the minds of these men or was seriously challenging them to enter the ministry. Whatever his intent, his words would soon come to pass.

In those days, the schoolhouses served as community centers for all types of occasions. It was here that Elias Sias preached his first sermon in the spring of 1859. The first time he offered an invitation, four individuals responded and were baptized by moonlight in the Pine River.[56]

A lumberman by the name of Bell from Sumner (Belltown) was in the audience during Elias' first sermon. Apparently he was impressed with what he heard, for he returned another time and told the group that he had announced to the Sumner community that Sias and Brooks would preach at Belltown. Shortly thereafter they obliged Mr. Bell's request, and in the spring of 1859, the Sumner congregation began.[57]

John Brown reveals the sincerity and determination of Elias' character, "he was so earnest in seeing sinners turn to the Lord that he

---

[54] Girdwood, Stone-Campbell, 52. Although the St. Louis and Coe church histories do not reflect this information, it is consistent with the local context and other historical information surrounding the congregations.
[55] Robinson, 3.
[56] This fact is noted in all the historical records.
[57] Brown, 251.

would start out early on the Lord's day to walk to different school houses and return home at ten o'clock, at night, after preaching four times and walking forty-three miles.[58]

Official Ordination

Elias was determined to find a stronger preacher for the congregation at Forest Hill. Several families with little children were walking six miles from St. Louis to the Forest Hill church. In the fall of 1859, Mr. Sias was determined to get some help for his congregation and others in the area.[59]

Elias heard about the Disciples' annual meeting that was being held in Toledo, Ohio (Fulton County). He decided to go to this meeting and ask for help for the churches in central Michigan. Elias walked from Forest Hill to Toledo, Ohio in the fall of 1859.[60]

Elias met L. L. Carpenter at the convention and persuaded him to return with him to Michigan; Mr. Carpenter agreed. The convention paid the train fares for the men to come as far as St. Johns. Mitchell Packer (son of A. V. Packer) met Elias and L. L. at the train station with ponies for the thirty mile journey north. Bob Girdwood adds a humorous note, "Carpenter was a tall man at 6'6" and the pony he rode left his feet dragging the ground at times."[61] Carpenter would later comment that "the boy led them through Indian trails, cow paths, and newly blazed trails" on their journey to Gratiot County.[62]

L. L. Carpenter stayed for awhile in central Michigan preaching to handfuls of people scattered throughout Gratiot and Isabella counties. It was during this time in 1861 while preaching in Salt River (Shepherd) that Mr. Carpenter ordained Elias and Elisha into the ministry. This officially marked the beginning of Elias' ministry where over 4,000 would be baptized and several congregations were started.[63]

It is important to note that there were no churches in Gratiot

---

[58] Ibid.
[59] Ibid.
[60] Meese, 5; Errett, 2; Brown, 251; Robinson, 3.
[61] Girdwood, Stone-Campbell, 50.
[62] Ibid.
[63] Ibid., 51.

County when Elias was baptized. Christianity was slowly entering the Michigan wilderness at that time. Within a few years, however, various denominational groups had established congregations in the prominent communities. Through the efforts of Elias Sias and Elisha Brooks, the Disciples would become one of the leading religious groups in the county. According to 2011 county statistics, the Independent Christian Churches and Churches of Christ are the third largest religious group represented in Gratiot County.

Conclusion

No one can question the sincerity of faith that was initially expressed at the Mourner's Bench in 1857. Elias and Amanda Sias truly wanted to be right with God when they answered the minister's call. Little did they know at that time that their decision would change the course of their lives and affect countless others in Michigan.

Elias' devotion to his newfound faith would propel him to the forefront of Christian leadership in central Michigan. His determination to share the gospel would take him all over the state. He would be regarded as Michigan's best evangelist.

CHAPTER 3

Evangelistic Work

When Elias "made a start"[64] at the Methodist meeting in the fall of 1858, no one at that time imagined he would become the most outstanding evangelist of his day in the state of Michigan. In May 1859 (eight months later) he preached his first sermon at Salt River (Shepherd). Perhaps like every first year preaching student he felt insecure in his efforts. Several years later in a March 29, 1884 Christian Standard article, Elias commented that "for six years he tried to preach."[65]

It is my opinion that Ben Soule's challenge to "prepare for the ministry" and because there were no Restoration preachers in the immediate vicinity, Elias felt compelled to take on the task of preaching the gospel in Gratiot County until someone better qualified could be secured. As early as 1861 Elias was joined by several partners. Initially, the group held meetings in Gratiot County, but eventually they expanded their ministry "to the north in the wilderness portion of Michigan establishing several churches."[66]

The first nine years of Elias' ministry were spent in Gratiot, Isabella, and Montcalm counties. In that time, he helped launch six congregations and an educational institution. As the Restoration brotherhood expanded in breadth and organization, soon Elias' ministry responsibilities would

[64] When an invitation response was made at such meetings in that day, it was called "making a start." Meese, 5.

[65] Girdwood, Stone-Campbell, 169.

[66] I do not have the exact citation of this quote, however it was recorded in "The American Christian Review," a publication of Benjamin Franklin (1856-1878).

also expand. The second nine years of ministry would be a time of recognition, prominence, and influence in brotherhood activities.

Michigan Christian Missionary Association

1849 was the beginning of structure and difficulty in the Disciples' movement. Alexander Campbell encouraged and supported the development of the American Christian Missionary Society.[67] He wanted the brotherhood to "found a general organization through which the entire brotherhood could cooperate to evangelize the world."[68] Early objection was reserved but grew in time. Those who objected to the Society believed that it was unscriptural and it replaced the individual congregation's responsibility.[69]

By the 1860's support for the Society was dwindling. It was apparent that a restructure was needed. The Louisville Plan offered to bring the needed structure to the supporting congregations.[70]

The Louisville Plan suggested that congregations send official delegates to district meetings; the districts would send delegates to a General Convention. Monies raised by congregations would be sent to the district. The district would keep half to employ state evangelists and send the other half to the state society. The state society would keep half of its money and send the other half to the General Convention.[71] This was the setting for the beginning of The Michigan Christian Missionary Association.

The first call for the organization of a Michigan Christian

---

[67] Garrison and DeGroot state that Alexander Campbell initially criticized the idea of societies but would become a "principle defender of the movement toward county, district, state, and eventually national organization." Winfred Ernest Garrison and Alfred T. DeGroot, The Disciples of Christ A History, (St. Louis: The Bethany Press, 1948), 234-236.

[68] Earl Irvin West, The Search For The Ancient Order, Vol. I, (Nashville: Gospel Advocate Company, 1974), 166.

[69] Ibid., 196.

[70] Lester G. McAllister & William E. Tucker, Journey In Faith A History Of The Christian Church (Disciples of Christ), (St. Louis: The Bethany Press, 1975), 257.

[71] Ibid., 257.

Missionary Association came in June 1868.[72] A notice was printed in the November Christian Standard that the first meeting would be held at the Jefferson Avenue church in Detroit. Officers were elected and the new organization represented 40 churches.[73] Elias and several other ministers from Michigan supported this effort.

A second meeting was held in Ionia on October 1, 1869. Elias Sias was elected to serve as recording secretary at this meeting. This began a thirteen year relationship between Elias and the Missionary Association.[74] The spirit of joy and hospitality experienced at the Ionia meeting was noted in the October 23 Christian Standard article.[75]

The third Association meeting was held at PawPaw in 1870. Elias is elected as the state corresponding secretary and 50 churches are represented at this meeting. At this meeting the State Association "unanimously adopts the uniform system" proposed by the Louisville Plan.[76] In August 1871, Elias announced in the Christian Standard that the third meeting would be held again at Ionia. He encouraged each congregation to take up a collection for the Association and send it along with two delegates to the meeting.[77]

The Plum Street congregation of Detroit hosted the fifth annual meeting in 1872. Although the congregation did not approve of the organization, they were willing to co-operate with the work it was trying to do.[78] Vernon Boyd explains the expectations of the District evangelists, "The Association divided the state into districts and employed evangelists for each: Elias Sias of Pine Run for District 1; J. H. Reese of Dowagiac for District 2; J. A. Mavity for District 3. Each man

---

[72] John Brown notes that the first general meeting looking toward co-operative work in the state happened in 1866, but the Michigan Society was not organized until 1868. Brown, 252.

[73] Girdwood, Stone-Campbell Movement, 74.

[74] Brown, 251.

[75] "Ionia Yearly Meeting," Christian Standard, (October 23, 1869): 340.

[76] Girdwood, Stone-Campbell Movement, 75. Girdwood also notes that in 1871 the Association attempted to develop a more effective and efficient organization by forming three districts.

[77] E. Sias, "Michigan Christian Missionary Convention," Christian Standard, Vol. VI, No. 33, (August 26, 1871): 269.

[78] R. Vernon Boyd, A History of The Stone-Campbell Churches in Michigan, N.P., N.P., (Southfield, 2009), 91.

was responsible for visiting the churches, raising funds for missionary work and reporting the results of their labors."[79]

Elias served as District evangelist at three periods for a total of thirteen years in the course of his ministry.[80] He was also asked to serve on the enrollment committee on Order of Business and Religious Exercises, which he did.[81] Although many in the Brotherhood had strong reservations about the Missionary Society, Elias did not and served its purpose from its beginning until his death.

1880 U. S. Census

The General Missionary Convention met at Bloomingdale, Illinois, October 23-26, 1879. In addition to the many issues on the Convention agenda, the group appointed to a committee five individuals "to collect statistics of our people and prepare a statement of them, to be inserted in the U. S. Census to be issued in 1880."[82] F. M. Green, J. B. Briney, R. Moffett, Elias Sias and L. L. Carpenter were the five men chosen to serve.[83]

The Sunday School Association

McAllister and Tucker note that Sunday school work furnished one of the first opportunities for cooperative work for the Disciples.[84] Although Alexander Campbell and Barton Stone were suspicious of the movement at first, by 1849 they encouraged the first national convention that same year.[85] The first International Sunday School Association, an interdenominational agency, led to the development of the first Uniform Lessons in 1872.[86]

---

[79] Ibid., 93

[80] Errett, "Sixty Miles to Be Baptized," 2. The evangelists were employed by the Association and unfortunately we do not know how much the evangelists were paid.

[81] Boyd, 92.

[82] General Missionary Convention, <u>Proceedings Of The General Christian Missionary Convention</u>, October 23-26, (Cincinnati, 1879): 12-13.

[83] Ibid.

[84] McAllister & Tucker, 278.

[85] Ibid.

[86] Ibid., 279

The Sunday school movement within the Disciples began in 1791.[87] By the 1849 General Convention in Cincinnati, J. T. Barclay suggested a better attempt at organizing Sunday schools in the brotherhood.[88] When talk grew among the churches in the ecumenical community of forming a uniform Sunday school movement, the Disciples were eager to be a part of it.[89] In addition to the International effort, many states developed their own Sunday school associations.

Although the details are brief, Elias was elected to the Executive Committee of the National Christian Sunday-School Association at Indianapolis, Indiana on August 8, 1884. The meeting was held at Bethany Park and reported in the Goshen Daily News and Decatur Morning Review.[90]

Washington D.C. Church Edifice Fund

According to an 1881 article in The Christian by J. H. Garrison, Elias served as the Michigan representative of the Washington D.C. Church Edifice Fund.[91] Unfortunately, no information that explains what this fund was exists.

Ministry Overview

Elias Sias preached the Gospel and shared the Restoration Movement principles for 46 years. In that time span he started fifteen churches, served in located ministry at eleven different congregations, and preached at numerous evangelistic meetings. Bob Girdwood has done an outstanding job of documenting Elias' ministry (along with others) in his book The Stone-Campbell Movement In Michigan. I would refer the interested reader to this work for specific details of Elias' ministry.

---

[87] James DeForest Murch, Christians Only, (Cincinnati: Standard Publishing, 1962), 34.

[88] Ibid., 149.

[89] According to Garrison and DeGroot, this is one area the Disciples "contributed with distinction" in the ecumenical world. 547.

[90] "Officers of the Sunday-School Association," Decatur Morning Review, August 8, 1884.

[91] J. H. Garrison, "State Agencies," The Christian, (January 27, 1881).

My purpose in the final pages of this chapter is not to reduplicate Bob's work, but to give a snapshot view of the extent of Elias' ministry. It is my hope that in seeing the scope of his ministry you can appreciate why he was called the greatest evangelist in the state of Michigan.

```
                    CHURCHES STARTED

    Pine River Nucleus Started          1858
        (Forest Hill, St. Louis, Coe)

    Sumner                              1859
    Shepherd                            1861
    Ferris                              1865
    The Christian Academy               1868
            (Helped Brooks start at St. Louis)

    Elm Hall                            1871
    Deanville                           1871
    Dowagiac                            1875
    Freemont                            1879
    Elba                                1879
    Cascade                             1880
    Pierson                             1880
    Saginaw                             1884
    Owosso (restart)                    1886
    Sanford                             1890
    Byron Center                        1891
```

Approximately half of the congregations started by Elias have closed.[92] Elm Hall closed in the same year it was started and was absorbed into area churches.[93] In addition to starting churches, Elias also served in several located ministries.

---

[92] Bob Girdwood states that many of these closures were the result of transitions in the lumber industry. In some instances entire towns moved to new locations. Girdwood, Restoration Movement, 6.

[93] Frank O. Kruger, The Origin and Development of the Churches of Christ (Disciples) in Michigan, 1835 to 1930, Thesis, (Butler University, 1949).

```
              EVANGELISTIC MEETINGS

     Forest Hill          1867
     Ferris               1868
     East Thetford        1869
     Wayland              1869
     Coldwater            1869
     Duplain              1870
     Fargo                1871
     Easton               1871
     Bloomingdale         1871
     Wakeshma             1875
     Silver Creek         1876
     Keeler               1876
     Dowagiac             1877
     Wayland              1877
     Galien               1879
     Petersburg           1879
     Pine Run             1879
     Bangor               1879
     Fremont              1880
     Pierson & Bailey     1880
     New Haven            1883
     Shepherd             1884
     Sumner               1886
     Pierson              1886
     Kalkaska             1889
     Solon Township       1893
     Belding              1904

     Occasional Preaching at Decatur 1886-1887
```

As state evangelist, Elias was expected to visit the established congregations to request financial support from them for the State Association and strengthen them as needed. From 1867-1904 he traveled east to west across the central part of Michigan and as far north as Kalkaska holding evangelistic meetings.

```
                  LOCATED MINISTRIES

     Begins preaching in Gratiot Co.      1859-1862
     Sumner                               1863
     St. Louis & Shepherd                 1864-1866
     Easton                               1871
     Clio                                 1872-1873
     Bloomingdale                         1873-1874
     Dowagiac                             1875-1877
     Cascade                              1881-1886
     Owosso                               1886-1887
     Wayland                              1887-1889
     St. Louis                            1891-1893
     Fremont                              1895-1898

     Retires                              1900

     Pulpit Supply                        1901-1905

     Wayland (lives remaining days)       1907-1911
```

Most of the preaching tours were conducted in between his located ministries while a few were held in close proximity to the congregations Elias served.

Elias was an exceptional communicator and organizer. He was able to enter a troubled church setting and bring healing. He could straighten out situations that seemed impossible but knew that he could not do it alone. In an 1886 Christian Standard report Elias lamented the need for more workers in Michigan,

> "The one great lack in our work here in Michigan is men of experience, full of faith to go out and reap and set in order. All that can be said of the great West as a fruitful field for work may be said of Michigan, especially the north half. The calls for help that are daily coming to me from different localities make me cry out, Lord of the harvest, send laborers into the fields which are already white. Much will be lost if the harvest wait. Disciples of Michigan, come to the rescue. Give time, money and prayers, that the good news of the gospel be spread abroad all over our State."[94]

Conclusion

In the early 1800's Elias Sias was a young man growing up in Ontario, Canada. He was full of hopes and dreams like most are and uncertain of the future. When his family moved to Michigan in search of work, the uncertainty increased. Michigan was an untamed, uncharted forest full of swamps and Indians.

Within four years of arriving in Michigan, Elias would find love and begin to make his mark in life. Two years later he would find God, and that event changed the course of his life. Elias was a committed Christian and wanted to share his faith with others. He did not have a Bible College education but became an outstanding preacher.

No one knows how many souls were reached through his efforts. It

---

[94] E. Sias, "Michigan," Christian Standard, (February 27, 1886), 70.

was said that he led 10,000 people to Christ in his lifetime.[95] Perhaps this was just the beginning as many more have benefitted from his ministry through the congregations he started.

At the bottom of the page is a visual map of Elias' ministry footprint. The crosses designate places where he started or helped to start a congregation. The stars indicate where he served in a located ministry or conducted an evangelistic meeting. I did not differentiate between ministries and meeting sites since several locations overlapped. My intent in printing the map is to give the reader a visual appreciation of the scope of Elias' work. The blank Michigan map is courtesy of www.myonlinemaps.com.

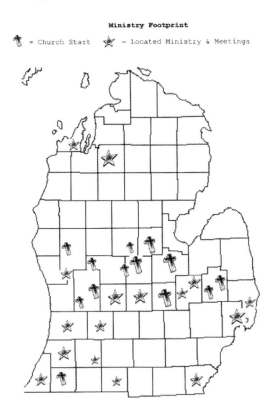

Ministry Footprint

✝ = Church Start ⭐ = Located Ministry & Meetings

---

[95] Boyd, 66. This is perhaps an exaggerated number as most histories report 4,000.

25

CHAPTER 4

Partners in Ministry

Elisha Brooks

No one was as big of help to Elias as was his neighbor and friend, Elisha Brooks. Elisha introduced Elias to the Restoration Movement; he let him borrow a horse to ride to Muir; and for ten years he partnered with Elias in starting new churches. These men were the prominent factor in bringing the Restoration Movement to central Michigan.

Elisha was born on April 4, 1819 in Braceville, Trumbull County, Ohio. He was the son of John and Hannah (Russell) Brooks.[96] At the age of 17, Elisha left his home in Braceville, Ohio to pursue employment.[97] He traveled and worked at various jobs. He married Laura J. Bartlett on April 9, 1845 in DeKalb County, Indiana. They were parents of eight children.

The discovery of gold in California in 1849 led Elisha to leave his family and join a wagon train westward in search of riches. When that endeavor failed, he returned home and eventually moved his family to Michigan.[98]

On October 10, 1854, Elisha purchased the NW quarter of section

---

[96] This information is on file at the Oak Grove Cemetery in St. Louis where Elisha was interred. Louise Davenport has also recorded an extensive look at Elisha's childhood based upon his diary in Academia On The Pine - The Landmark That Was Yerington's College, (St. Louis: The Gratiot County Historical Society, 1981).
[97] Coe Church of Christ history records details of his early life. Darryl Quidort, A History of Coe Church of Christ - Sesquicentennial 1863-2013, (St. Louis, 2013).
[98] Ibid.

1 (160 acres), Pine River township for $80.00 (one mile east and one mile south of Coe). The family moved to Maple Rapids, Clinton county until the log cabin was completed.[99] In the spring of 1855 he moved his wife and two children to his homestead where they built a home and cleared the land for farming. This homestead bordered the Sias homestead to the south.[100]

Like his friend Elias, Elisha ran for local public office. He was elected as Justice of the Peace in 1857. He applied for a Post Office branch at his home, 4 miles north of that settlement, to serve local residents. He was appointed Postmaster (February 24, 1857 to June 17, 1859) and named that Post Office, "Forest Hill," a description of his hilltop home. Thereafter, the branch office was passed to homes of other Postmasters until it came to rest at a small settlement 5 miles south west of where it started (now Forest Hill).[101]

The Forest Hill Post Office was eventually located across the road from the Christian Church. The church building in this picture was the original building built in 1897. Although damaged by fire and wind, the original structure is still in use. (Picture reprint from Tucker's history of Gratiot County, 1127). Public domain.>

No one knows when Elisha became a Christian. It is highly probable that this event happened at Newville, Indiana after he returned from California.[102] He was a member of the Disciples and the congregation at Newville before coming to Michigan. It is also likely that Elisha

---

[99] This information was obtained from Warren Brooks' obituary (Elisha's son). St. Louis Historical Society.

[100] Quidort. See Gratiot County map in chapter one.

[101] History of Gratiot County attributes the Forest Hill name to Elisha Brooks. Tucker, 1126.

[102] Elisha was acquainted with Randal Faurot the minister of the Christian Church at Newville. Meese, 5.

had received the tract "Sincerity Seeking The Way To Heaven" from Randal Faurot.

When Elisha heard the news that Elias and Amanda had "made a start" at the Methodist meeting, he shared Benjamin Franklin's tract with Elias.[103] Within a year the two men would be engaged in evangelistic endeavors in central Michigan. From 1859 through 1869 Elisha and Elias preached at school houses in St. Louis, Shepherd, Mt. Pleasant, Sumner, Elm Hall and Ferris. They parted company in 1869 as Elias began to pursue wider brotherhood interests.

Elisha spent 35 years preaching in Gratiot and surrounding counties. It is believed that he baptized 1,000 and helped start numerous congregations. According to his personal diary, "his eldest daughter, Jessie, often accompanied him, playing a guitar and singing gospel music."[104] The Christian Banner described Elisha as "an able expounder of the gospel; bold to take up, and firm to sustain, the gospel of Christ."[105]

Mr. Brooks was acquainted with the hardships and discouragement of ministry. He wrote a brief letter describing his work to the Christian Standard in 1873,

> "Since my last report, I have spent some time laboring in Clinton Co., and have gathered up and organized twenty-two members in the Hammond neighborhood, and eight more in Bengal, with a prospect of a goodly number more in each place, if the Lord should permit me to labor more there. But I have twice been called home from there by sickness in my family which resulted each time in the death of one of our dear children which leaves us sadly broken up in earth's dearest hopes. It sometimes seems as if the providence of God were

---

[103] Bob Girdwood wrote a historical novel account of what he thinks may have happened when the Brooks and Sias families met. With permission, I have reprinted this in Appendix B.

[104] Davenport, Academia On The Pine, no page numbers given.

[105] I do not have the exact citation, but the quote came from John R. Howard, Christian Banner (October 11, 1890).

against my laboring there. But our loss is the eternal gain of the dear one gone."[106]

Elisha Brooks passed away on September 19, 1891.[107] L. L. Carpenter reported his death as occurring at five o'clock. "He was in the house with his family, sitting in a chair, talking with his wife, when he suddenly exclaimed, O! and expired immediately without even a struggle. He died of heart disease."[108] Carpenter went on to say about Brooks, "he has been a preacher of the pure gospel. He clearly understood the gospel of Christ. He believed it with all his heart, and no man was more loyal to it than was Bro. Brooks."[109]

The St. Louis Academy

In 1865 (or perhaps earlier) Elisha Brooks wanted to start a Christian Academy. The purpose of the Academy was to promote and teach Disciples' principles.[110] At the encouragement of Randal and Letitia Faurot, Elisha began his project in 1865.[111]

The St. Louis Academy Association was formed and Elisha was designated as president.[112] Elias Sias, William Leonard, and a Professor Fowler joined in the effort with Mr. Brooks.[113] They began to solicit funds for the Academy and soon had enough to erect a large frame building.[114] A parcel of land was purchased on the north bank of the

---

[106] E. H. Brooks, "Michigan," <u>Christian Standard</u>, Vol. VIII, No. 15, (April 12, 1873), 119.

[107] See Appendix D "BROOKS" for an extended look at his life as recorded in his personal diary.

[108] L. L. Carpenter, "BROOKS," <u>Christian Standard</u>, (November 12, 1890), 17.

[109] Ibid.

[110] The Disciples firmly believed that "the establishment of institutions in which learning might be fostered and by which it might be disseminated" was essential. Garrison and DeGroot, 223.

[111] Davenport. No page numbers were printed on the booklet "Academia On The Pine." It is not certain when the Faurots came to Michigan. A June 1914 <u>Christian Banner</u>, article suggests they may have come to Michigan in 1858 at the request of Brooks and Sias.

[112] Ibid.

[113] Howard, <u>Christian Banner</u>, November 1923.

[114] Robinson, 4.

Pine River in downtown St. Louis.[115] While the building was being enclosed, a cyclone struck the building, breaking and scattering many of the timbers. Construction was resumed and the east wing was completed first.[116]

By the fall of 1866, the Academy was not completed but classes could begin.[117] The Faurots sold their property in Newville, Indiana and moved to St. Louis to launch the Academy. In April 1868, Mr. Faurot solicited help in acquiring hymnals for the Academy in the May 9, 1868 Christian Standard. He also expressed the hope of having the Academy completed and ready for the fall term.[118]

Randal and Letitia Faurot

Randal Faurot was the minister of the Disciples church at Newville, Indiana. He was Elisha's minister and Newville was his home church. It is not surprising that Elisha would rely upon his mentor in the early years of his ministry. When Elisha had expressed the desire to begin an Academy in St. Louis, the Faurots were more than willing to help out.

Randal and Letitia were educators who loved teaching. "Before coming to St. Louis they had founded parochial schools in other Michigan communities as well as in Indiana, Ohio and the South."[119] The Faurots remained in St. Louis until the Academy was well established but left for Jackson, Mississippi in 1881 where they helped with the relocation of the Southern Christian Institute.[120]

Randal died on October 10, 1882 from typhoid fever and was

---

[115] Meese, 6.

[116] Robinson, 4.

[117] M. Riddle in an October 1867 Christian Standard commented that "Bro. Brooks is trying to get an Academy started in St. Louis; it is already raised but not completed." M. Riddle, "Correspondence," Christian Standard, Vol. 2, No. 43, (October 11, 1867): 341.

[118] R. Faurot, "Michigan," Christian Standard, Vol. III, No. 30, (Cincinnati: May 9, 1868): 149. For additional biographical information, see Appendix E.

[119] Davenport, "Academia On The Pine." Brown writes that Randall got sick due to "excess labors" in repairing the school's buildings. His grave was made on a "tree-crowned knoll." Brown, 169.

[120] Girdwood, Stone-Campbell Movement, 139. Brown shows several pictures of the first buildings of the Institute, Brown, 172-175.

buried on the campus of the Institute.[121] He was not able to see the Institute become the "only high-grade industrial college for the colored people" in its day.[122] The Institute had a faculty of thirteen, and an enrollment of 223 students.[123] Garrison and DeGroot state that "the actual operation of this school was begun by Letitia."[124]

Due to Randal's untimely death, Mrs. Faurot needed help. W. A. Belding came to her aid and eventually the Institute was taken over by the Christian Women's Board of Missions.[125] Letitia remained with the Institute for six years.[126] She moved to California in 1889 and returned to St. Louis in 1893 to live out her remaining years and when she died, by her own request, she was buried in an unmarked grave in Oakgrove Cemetery.[127]

The Academy as it looked in its original form. Picture reprint from Academia On The Pine, used with permission.

The Academy operated for 20 years but interest eventually lagged and enrollment dropped off significantly. LouiseDavenport surmises

---

[121] Ibid.

[122] M. M. Davis, How the Disciples Began and Grew, "Phillips Bible Institute Series," (Cincinnati: Standard Publishing Company, 1915), 174.

[123] Ibid.

[124] Garrison and DeGroot, 478.

[125] Girdwood, Stone-Campbell Movement, 139.

[126] Elias Sias, "Faurot," Christian Standard, (October 12, 1901), 30. Brown says she stayed with the Institute for two years (p. 169).

[127] Davenport, "Academia On The Pine." $1,000.00 was sent to the Institute at Letitia's death. Brown, 169.

that the decline in interest was due to a new Grammar School that opened in 1877 in downtown St. Louis. The Christian Academy closed its doors in 1881. The property was sold in 1890 and eventually another college was opened on the site.[128]

Ministry Overview

Elisha's ministry was not as prolific as Elias', however, he is credited with starting or helping to start several congregations in central Michigan. The chart below lists churches that Elisha was instrumental in starting.

```
                    CHURCHES STARTED

        Pine River Nucleus Started       1858
             (Forest Hill, St. Louis, Coe)

        Sumner (with Sias)               1859
        Shepherd                         1861

        The Christian Academy            1868

        Duplain                          1868
        Deanville (with Sias)            1871
        Bengal                           1873
        Hammond                          1873
        Pierson (with Sias)              1876
        Goss                             1877
        Pierson (with Sias)              1880
```

Elisha served as state Evangelist in 1875[129] but unlike Elias, he stayed close to home. The substance of his ministry was conducted primarily in Gratiot county. It is stated in Warren Brooks' obituary, that his father continued to farm the homestead until his death. Over the years he would return to the congregations he helped start to hold evangelistic meetings and offer encouragement to the members.

After Elisha's death in 1891, Laura lived with their youngest

---

[128] Charles Yerington purchased the Academy property in 1890 and opened Yerington's College. Davenport, "Academy On The Pine." Picture courtesy of Gratiot County Historical Society.

[129] Girdwood, The Stone-Campbell Movement, 127.

child, Nellie and her husband, on their farm that was adjacent to the homestead, until the day she died. Laura Brooks passed away on April 6, 1908 at the age of 79 and was buried along side of her husband at Oak Grove Cemetery in St. Louis.

Conclusion

In addition to his ministry accomplishments, there are three significant historical achievements that Elisha Brooks will be remembered for.

The first achievement is his introduction of Benjamin Franklin's tract to Elias Sias. Sincerity Seeking The Way To Heaven changed Elias' life and subsequently his. Without that tract, he and Elias may have never been nothing more than pioneer farmers in Gratiot County. As noble as that occupation is, farming would not have enabled them to affect the thousands of lives that the ministry did. Consequently, the Restoration Movement would not have impacted central Michigan as early as it did without Elisha sharing that tract one day with his neighbor Elias Sias.

Another achievement Elisha will be remembered for is the name Forest Hill. If Elisha had not exerted his influence in requesting to be the first postmaster of his little village and had he not chosen the name Forest Hill after looking out over his property, the community that exists there today might have as easily been named Moodyville or Gates Town after another prominent pioneer family. Although the community is not as large as it was in the early years, it is still named Forest Hill.

Finally, the college on the hill in down town St. Louis operated as the Christian Academy from 1866-1881 and later more notably as Yerington's College. The building stood vacant for many years after the college closed and was finally razed in 1952. Many today are oblivious to its once famed existence. However, in the annals of St. Louis, Michigan, Elisha Brooks is given credit for building and starting the Academy on the hill.

In his own unique way, Elisha Brooks made valuable contributions to the community where he lived. He was a farmer, educator, civil servant, and preacher of the Gospel. In contrast to his younger years, he never traveled far from his home. His influence, however, would impact many throughout the State of Michigan.

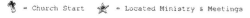

Elisha's Ministry Footprint

✝ = Church Start   ✷ = Located Ministry & Meetings

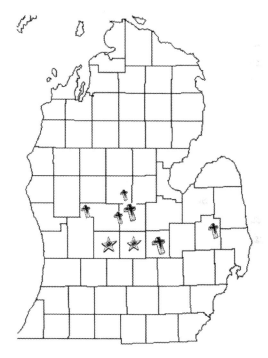

CHAPTER 5

Later Years

Personal Tragedy

1873 was a busy year for Elias. He served on the Michigan Christian Missionary Society enrollment committee. He was chosen as the District #1 evangelist. He dedicated a new building at Ionia and moved from Pine Run to Bloomingdale.

Amidst the business of ministry demands, there was also personal tragedy. Ministers are accustomed to caring for others who experience hardship and occasionally experience it as well. Tragedy came to the Sias home in May 1873 with the death of three children. J. Hurd reported the tragedy in the August 16, 1873 <u>Christian Standard,</u>

> "Our beloved Brother and Sister Sias, of Bloomingdale, Mich., have been deeply afflicted during the past spring. Three of their lovely family were carried to the cold grave by the hand of death. Little Elma, aged one year, and little Maud, aged 3 years and one month, died on the 9th of May; and on the 11th their little forms were gently laid away side by side in the same grave. On the 13th of the same month, their little daughter, Lola A., also fell asleep in death, aged 13 years and 4 months. We were present at her burial on the 14th following. Their disease was pneumonia bronchitis. Bro. Sias had just moved his family from Pine Run to Bloomingdale,

to labor for the church at the latter place. What untried sorrows came to that new home! But they sorrow not as those that have no hope."[130]

What wonderful sentiments expressed by Mr. Hurd. I cannot fathom the pain of losing one child let alone three in one month. The grief of the Sias family must have been tremendous. I am sure that the presence of Mr. Hurd, along with others, helped comfort the Sias family in their time of loss.

From East To West

The first fifteen years of ministry (1859-1873) Elias spent primarily in Gratiot, Isabella, and Montcalm Counties. He and fellow ministry partners preached in area schoolhouses and established several churches. With the exception of a two year ministry in Pine Run (Genesee County) 1871 to early 1873, Elias remained close to his home in St. Louis.

While ministering at Pine Run, Elias preached at several locations in western Michigan and becomes aware of strife in many congregations. He laments that the Union City congregation closed "due to internal strife and discouragement and there are many like that in Michigan."[131]

In March 1873, Elias moves his family from St. Louis to Bloomingdale. This would begin an eventful and tragic year for Elias. The move to Bloomingdale would also indicate a significant shift in ministry location. He would spend the next twenty-five years of ministry (1873-1898) on the western side of the state, and remain there until his death.

Wayland would become the chief operating base from which Elias would work. He ministered at St. Louis in 1891 and Fremont in 1895 but returned to Wayland after each short term ministry. It is possible that Elias served as a circuit riding preacher during this time. The old Forest Hill church records state that he relieved William Moody in

---

[130] J. Hurd, "DIED," Christian Standard, August 16, 1873 (Cincinnati: Standard Publishing, 1873): 261.
[131] E. Sias, "Union City," May 6, 1871, (Cincinnati: Christian Standard, 1871).

1891. Elias would serve the Lord for seventeen years on the west side of the state before things began to change for him personally.

Slowing Down

No one knows how it happened, but an October 30, 1890 issue of The Christian Evangelist reported that Elias had to have three fingers amputated and was doing as well as possible.[132] Within two and a half years, on April 9, 1893, he would suffer a paralytic stroke that took six months to recover from.[133] He would return to work in November of 1893, but the volume of his work over the next five years would drastically diminish. Elias made one more ministry change to Fremont in 1895 and back to Wayland one final time in 1898.

Retirement

Elias retired from full time ministry at Wayland in 1899.[134] He would find unspecified secular work and pulpit supply until 1905. He served one more time as the Correspondence Secretary for Michigan and attended the National Convention in Cincinnati in 1903. At the convention, Elias pledged to find fifty subscriptions for the Christian Standard from Michigan.[135] Mrs. Sias noted her husband's devotion to the publication from the beginning as he was "present when it was first arranged for Christian Standard to be published and was a weekly visitor ever since."[136]

Elias attended the "Muir Semi-centennial" in 1906 at the age of 72. Many prominent past members and ministers attended the event and joyfully reminisced. It was reported that the most interesting incident

---

[132] J. H. Garrison, The Christian Evangelist, October 30, 1890, (Missouri: Christian Publishing Company, 1890).

[133] "Stroke," Christian Standard, October 14, 1893, (Cincinnati: Standard Publishing Company, 1893).

[134] Disciples of Christ, District Year Book 1900, (Indianapolis: Disciples of Christ, 1900), 20.

[135] "Cincinnati," Christian Standard, May 20, 1903, (Cincinnati: Standard Publishing Company, 1903).

[136] Disciples of Christ, District Year Book 1910, (Indianapolis: Disciples of Christ, 1910), 109.

was the recital by Elias of his conversion experience. He described how his conversion brought the "transformation of a whole unbelieving and wicked neighborhood."[137] It was lamented that his testimony was not recorded word for word, however, Elias promised to write out the story for the Standard readers.[138] It is probable that this promise was never fulfilled.

Funeral For A Friend

Randal Faurot died and was buried on the campus of Southern Christian Institute in 1882. Upon the death of her husband, Letitia moved to California in 1889 to live with her sister.[139] She returned to St. Louis, Michigan in 1893 where she lived out the remainder of her days among family.[140] Mrs. Faurot passed away on August 17, 1901, "by her own request, she was buried in a little known spot in an unmarked grave in Oakgrove Cemetery."[141]

Louise Davenport writes that according to tradition,

> "Michigan visitors to the Institute in later years found that the faculty and students had revered the founders of their school by hanging their portraits in the administration building and by carefully tending the grave site with its two markers, very few ever realizing that only one person was buried there. Letitia had reasoned that, no matter where her earthly body was laid, her heart and soul would be beside Randall's and so, before leaving Mississippi, she had her own stone placed beside that of her husband."[142]

---

[137] "Muir Semi-centennial," Christian Standard, September 29, 1906, (Cincinnati: Standard Publishing Company, 1906): 3.

[138] Ibid.

[139] Sias, "Faurot," 30.

[140] Davenport, no page number available.

[141] Ibid.

[142] Ibid.

Elias assisted in the funeral of his longtime friend and partner in ministry in November 1901.[143]

His Death

The Christian Standard article from Muir noted that Elias' "bodily infirmities has limited his activity as a minister of the Word, but his mind is clear and his spirit is eager."[144] In June 1910, he suffered a "severe illness"[145] that would sideline him until his death, ten months later on April 5, 1911. The official cause of death was Paralysis Agitans (Parkinson's Disease).

I record his obituary as it was originally printed in the newspaper,

> "On Apr. 5, 1911, the spirit of E. Sias of Wayland, passed to his reward. Here was a man of unusual attainments, who left the farm and the woods to carry the riches of the gospel to the people. He was always a man of the people. He spoke the language of the people. He spoke to the hearts of the people, and in a pioneer country, when people were scarce, he baptized 4,432 candidates. For fifteen years he was our Michigan State evangelist. He was a great preacher by nature, and grace added to his strength. He built or organized fifteen churches in Michigan. He preached nearly fifty years. Surely many can arise and call him blessed. His later years were spent in Wayland, where he fell asleep. F. P. Arthur, now the State evangelist of Michigan, conducted the funeral service, assisted by the minister, Fay Wing, and on April 8 he was laid away with five of his children in the Bloomingdale Cemetery.
>
> He was married at St. Louis, Mich., in 1855, to Amanda Clymer. There were ten children: five are

---

[143] Disciples of Christ, District Year Book 1901, (Indianapolis: Disciples of Christ, 1901), 15.

[144] "Muir Semi-centennial," 3.

[145] Disciples of Christ, District Year Book 1910, (Indianapolis: Disciples of Christ, 1910), 109.

now living and five are at rest. His faithful and devoted wife is living in Wayland, and counts it a great joy to remember all she suffered and did for him in his life, and especially during the last few years. His mind and body gradually gave way and his glad release came.

Michigan has been honored by great preachers, but among them all, for an Elijah-like spirit, Elias Sias stood high. It was our brother's wish that his brethren should place a headstone at his grave, and I am now collecting a fund for that purpose. Send all offerings for the fund to F. P. Arthur, Grand Rapids, Mich."[146]

Amanda would live for another thirteen years before passing away on March 16, 1924 at Port Huron. She was buried next to her husband at the family plot in Bloomingdale. According to the Sias family history, most of their family is buried there.[147]

---

[146] I do not have the source of the obituary, it was provided to me by the Disciples of Christ Historical Society in Nashville, Tennessee.

[147] Sias, 112.

Ministry In Canada

It is easy to understand how some dates can be errantly recorded when comparing multiple accounts of an historical narrative. It is harder to justify some events when there is no correlation between stated facts. This is the case with regard to Elias' supposed ministry in Canada.

Elias' parents moved their family to Ontario from New York briefly when he was a child. Two of his siblings were born there and the family moved to Michigan when he was sixteen. Sylvenus would move his family a final time to Pine River township in 1854. These facts are undisputed.

There are two statements in the Sias family history concerning Elias' ministry that are hard to substantiate with the time line of his life. The first statement is made in a biographical family note describing who Elias was, "He preached in many places in Michigan and Canada," writes Azariah Sias.[148]

The second statement is a conversation recorded between two Sias family members in a letter dated August 19, 1924. Charles A. Sias, from Oregon, wrote to his cousin, Edgar Sias who resided in Forest Hill, Michigan. Charles is responding to Edgar's question about family history. Charles tells Edgar that he wrote to Elias Sias of Wayland, a preacher of the N.T. faith, who was well along in years at that time. According to Charles, Elias said, "He said he knew little of his family, as he had drifted into Canada when quite young, and had not been in touch with his folks on his return."[149]

The difficulty with these two statements is that there is no way to justify them with the time line of his life. Once his family moved to Michigan from Ontario there is nothing to suggest that Elias was ever in Canada again. There is nothing recorded in his ministry events that could even remotely allow for any time of ministry in Canada. His father and uncle Solomon Jr. brought their families to Pine River township and settled there until their deaths. Elias would have had constant contact with his family for many years.

What are we to make of these apparent contradictions? I will let the

---

[148] Sias, 112.
[149] Ibid., 438.

reader make their own conclusions. My intent is to simply report what has been recorded. I have no way of correlating these statements with known events, so I will let them stand alone.

Tidbits And Reflections

Elias had a positive impact upon people everywhere he went. This was not only seen in the success of his ministries but also in the comments that others made about him. In what follows are tidbits of information and comments made about Elias that I have uncovered in articles, church histories, and other publications.

Easton Church of Christ - 1877

Elias was the second minister of Easton and highly revered by the congregation. On September 17, 1877, the cornerstone of the building was laid. An historical sketch of the church and a New Testament carried and used by Elias Sias for nine years were deposited in the cornerstone as well as the names of eighty-nine persons who had contributed one dollar each toward the building.[150]

Cascade Christian Church - 1864

Elias helped start this congregation and was its first minister. At their Centennial celebration in 1964 church members described him as "a remarkable man and a heroic Christian - self educated but gifted." Fay Wing, Disciple minister who was a boy in the church at that time said Elias "preached wonderful sermons, which made people think, and that he liked to fish."[151]

---

[150] Easton church history printed for their 125th Anniversary, 2.
[151] Cascade Christian Church, "Open Doors, Open Hearts, Open Minds," Centennial Issue (1864-1964), 5

Salt River (Shepherd) - 1884

Upon returning to Cascade Christian Church after holding a meeting at the Salt River congregation in March 1884, Elias reminisced about his early days with the church at Shepherd.

> "My first effort to preach the gospel was there. It was there I was ordained to the work, and in weakness and trembling for about six years tried to preach for them. To go back to these old friends of labor, meet with the tried and true of other days, talk over the battles of the past, victories won through faith in Christ, and the hopes of the future, are my richest experiences in this journey to the land beyond."[152]

Owosso Church of Christ - 1866

In 1866 Elias was sent to Owosso to restart the congregation after its closure due to internal conflicts as result of the Civil War. Not only did he go there to preach the gospel but helped build a new building. The church history records that Elias proceeded to gather material for the building. Stone for the foundation was hauled to the Pine Street lot. Mr. Sias aided in the cutting of the timber for the building.[153]

Comments In Publications

October 30, 1890 Christian Evangelist article proclaimed Elias, "one of the most faithful and efficient preachers in Michigan."

June 11, 1910 Christian Standard article said Elias was, "one of Michigan's early state evangelist and most untiring workers."

November 1923 Christian Banner exclaims, "in his day he was the most powerful speaker in Michigan."[154]

---

[152] E. Sias, "Cascade," Christian Standard, Vol. XIX, No. 13, March 29, 1884, (Cincinnati: Standard Publishing Company, 1884): 102.

[153] Park H. Netting, Velma Morehouse, and Uldene LeRoy, A History of the First Church of Christ, Owosso, Michigan, 2014.

[154] These articles were cited elsewhere and were simply reiterated here for emphasis.

Ferris Church of Christ - 1944

Elias helped start the Ferris congregation in 1865. There are two articles printed about his ministry with this congregation that could perhaps describe the setting everywhere he went. The 2003 revision of the church history records how elderly members recalled their parents' tales of Elias, "In the past, older members recalled their parents telling of men of the church carrying New Testaments in their pockets as they worked in the fields, and while resting the oxen, reading to see whether the things Elder Sias preached were true."[155]

Mrs. Mary Thompson

My favorite article was recorded in a September 23, 1944 <u>Christian Standard</u> article. Mrs. Mary Thompson, an elderly member of Ferris, recalls her childhood experience with Elias Sias. Nine year old Mary Bailey heard Elias preach the gospel at Ferris Center and she wanted to be baptized. For some unknown reason she was not baptized at that time.

It was not until she was fourteen that Mary Bailey was baptized, when Elias preached at the "yearly meeting" at Sumner. Mrs. Thompson continued to describe her childhood fondly as consisting of Indians pitching wigwams near her home and white neighbors who came to hear the gospel preached at Ferris Center.[156]

The picture at the right of the page was taken of Mrs. Thompson many years later while she attended a meeting at Rock Lake Christian Assembly. It was first printed in a September 23, 1944 <u>Christian Standard</u> article. Permission to reprint the photo was given by her family.

---

[155] "The Church by the Side of the Road," <u>History Of The Ferris Church Of Christ</u>, August 22, 2003, 2.

[156] "Memories of Early Days in Michigan," <u>Christian Standard</u>, September 23, 1944, (Cincinnati: Standard Publishing Company, 1944): 6.

J. D. Murch - 1961

Restoration author, James DeForest Murch described Elias as "the state's most successful evangelist, winning thousands to Christ."[157]

William R. Sias - 1899

Perhaps it is best to close this section with a fond remembrance of a family member from that era. William Sias was a cousin of Elias and recalls his visit to their home in Mt. Pleasant, "Elias was a minister of the Disciple Church. In 1899 he came to Mt. Pleasant, Michigan, where we lived, to preach the funeral sermon of the brother minister of that church. He came to visit my father and spent the night at our house. He was a very likeable person."[158] No doubt a sentiment shared by many people who knew him.

Conclusion

I do not know how long Elias suffered with Parkinson's Disease or to what extent it eventually led to his death. It is probable that the stroke he experienced in 1893 was the onset of this disease. Regardless the diagnosis, Elias' spirit was not diminished. He continued to find ways to serve God until it was physically impossible.

The unsung hero of this story is Amanda Sias. She moved all over central Michigan with her husband. Many times she was home alone with the children while Elias traveled. She endured the loss of three children in one month and ultimately became a care giver to her husband in the final years of his life.

Elias and Amanda Sias are distinct examples of faithfulness. From the moment they pledged their lives to God on that fall evening in 1857, they served him in their own unique ways until the end of their lives.

---

[157] James DeForest Murch, <u>Christians Only</u>, (Cincinnati: Standard Publishing Company, 1961), 126.

[158] Sias, 112.

CHAPTER 6

Lasting Impact

The Apostle John wrote, "Then I heard a voice from heaven say, "Write this: Blessed are the dead who die in the Lord from now on." "Yes," says the Spirit, "they will rest from their labor, for their deeds will follow them."[159] Millennial theologians argue over the exegesis of this verse, however, the basic understanding is obvious, any life lived for Christ will continue to have an earthly impact long after that life is over.

I did not know Elias Sias. I have never met anyone from his family. He passed from this life over a hundred years ago. The congregation I serve began the year he died. Although Elias had nothing to do with the beginning of East Superior Christian Church directly, indirectly he did. Members of the congregations he started shared a vision of starting a Restoration congregation in Alma; that vision became a reality in 1911.

Given the nature and length of his illness, it is doubtful that Elias was ever aware of the Alma congregation. Current members of East Superior have never heard of Elias Sias and many members of the area churches have no awareness of him either. Regardless of our ignorance, we are products of his labor and our existence is a testimony to his sacrifice.

The object of this project from the outset has been to give a personal glimpse of Elias Sias. Nothing of depth has ever been definitively written about him. What has been written are scattered pieces of information spanning the scope of his life. It is astounding to me that this man who played a major role in the establishment of so many Restoration

---

[159] Rev. 14:13 (New International Version)

movement congregations in central Michigan is only acknowledged in simple sentence statements.

What have we learned in this project about Elias Sias? Most importantly, he and his wife were people of sincere faith. From the beginning of their profession of faith in Jesus Christ they were determined to share their faith with those who were close to them. That passion became a lifelong occupation.

Elias had no formal theological training or practical ministry experience, yet he was a gifted leader. He had the unique ability to come into a troubled situation, set things in order and leave that particular congregation in better condition than when he arrived.

Although he never attended a Bible College, Elias was a student of the Bible. It is evident in his conversion experience that he was willing to read and learn. I am confident, because of that fact, when Elias considered the notion of preaching he researched how to prepare and deliver a sermon. I am also confident that he studied the ministers who came to help him in his work. Perhaps he received some early instruction from his educator friend, Randall Faurot.

Elias' preaching style was down to earth. F. P. Arthur eloquently noted in his obituary, Elias was "a man of the people. He spoke the language of the people. He spoke to the hearts of the people." That is a model for every ministry student to emulate.

It is hard to ascertain Elias' specific personality characteristic from the scant information available. However, initial observation leads me to conclude that he was probably a Type-A personality. I base this conclusion upon the following facts: he was a self-starter, he was determined, goal oriented, outgoing and personable. These qualities are characteristic of this particular personality type.

I do not know how many of the Restoration founding fathers he met. Barton Stone had already passed away in 1844 and Walter Scott died in 1861. Considering Elias' involvement in many of the brotherhood activities, it is very likely that he met Alexander Campbell some time before his death in 1868. All this, of course, is conjecture on my part. What is not conjecture, is Elias' dedication to Restoration movement principles. This is evident throughout his ministry.

What is the lasting impact of his life and ministry? Elias is credited with starting and/or helping to start fifteen plus churches in the span of forty years. Approximately half of those congregations are alive and functioning well at present. Some of those congregations died early as the communities they existed in died. Some died because of constant internal struggles that could never be completely repaired. Others simply changed from their origin as the movement splintered and changed shortly after Elias' death.

I have no doubt that the Sias children were raised in a Godly home. What became of their faith in adulthood is not known. Most of Elias and Amanda's children stayed close to home and eventually died there. The Siases were privileged to witness the birth of all six of their grandchildren born in the late 1800's, giving them ample time to dote.

Elias' brother Lucian stayed close to the homestead and raised his family there. His descendants had a lasting impact upon the St. Louis and Forest Hill congregations. Great grandson, Max R. Sias, served as Deacon, Trustee, and Secretary-Treasure of the Sunday school and was chosen to serve as chairman of the building committee of the St. Louis congregation. Many of Lucian's descendants were active members of the St. Louis Church of Christ through the 1950's.[160] Only a small number of the Sias family members currently attend the St. Louis congregation and reside in Gratiot County. However, most are gone due to death and dispersion.

The Bible teaches that we should "give honor to whom honor is due."[161] It was my intent in writing this book to honor Elias Sias the man. His church planting exploits are documented well in <u>Christian Standard</u> articles and Bob Girdwood's book <u>The Stone-Campbell Movement In Michigan</u>. Young, aspiring ministers would do well to note his ministry style and emulate it. Church members could impact their communities with the passion and determination that Elias exhibited in his life.

It is my hope that in reading about this pioneer church planter you have gained an understanding of the vision that fueled a movement in nineteenth century America and lit a fire in the heart of Elias Sias. This fire was also shared by several of his family members. Charles A. Sias,

---

[160] Azariah Boody Sias, <u>The Sias Family In America 1677-1952</u>, Vol. III, Supplement 2, (Orlando: Florida Press, 1967), 48.

[161] Romans 13:7 (New International Version)

distant relative of Elias and Disciples minister, sums up the motivation of the Restoration movement and Elias' passion,

> "The plea for the restoration of the N.T. church has appealed to me since my conversion when 20. Its contrast with the isms of the world is so strong, that I am strongly opposed to any tendency to ecclesiasticism, or in any sense the denominationalizing of "The Way." The old plea and the old book for me."[162]

---

[162] Sias, Vol. I, 439.

APPENDIX A

Sincerity Seeking the Way to Heaven

By
Benjamin Franklin[163]

BENJAMIN FRANKLIN.

First Printing 1856
Place of publication & publisher not identified
Reprint:
Cincinnati: Chase & Hall, 1875

---

[163] Benjamin Franklin was a second generation Restoration preacher and outstanding publisher. He wrote <u>SINCERITY SEEKING THE WAY TO HEAVEN</u> in 1856. I have reproduced the document exactly as it was published by Franklin. The picture was reprinted from John T. Brown, <u>Churches of Christ</u>, (Louisville: John P. Morton And Company, 1904), 421. Public domain.

CHRISTIAN EXPERIENCE

SINCERITY SEEKING THE WAY TO HEAVEN

BY BENJAMIN FRANKLIN.

CHAPTER I.

SINCERITY, a young man of twenty-one years, awoke one morning, and soliloquized with himself thus: "I have now arrived at manhood, and feel surprised when I think that twenty-one years of my life have fled, and I have not made the first effort to seek God. I am astonished at myself that I have lived this long without God, and without hope. I will remain in this condition no longer. If there is a man in this town who can show me the way to heaven, I will enter upon it before the setting of another sun. I will immediately cross the way to the residence of Mr. H., the Presiding Elder of the M. E. Church, an excellent man, who will readily show me the way to heaven." In a few minutes our young friend was rapping at the door of Mr. H. "Walk in," responded from within. "Good morning, Mr. S.." said the good man, "I trust I see you well." "Quite well, Mr. H., in body, but I have much concern of mind. I am, sir, alarmed when I think that twenty-one years of my life are gone, and 1 am not a *Christian!* I have, therefore, called upon you as a friend, to show me what I must do to be saved."

Honesty. Do you desire that I should pray for you?

Sincerity. I am ignorant of the way of salvation. I desire you to point out what the Lord requires me to do, that I may be saved. If it is for you to pray for me, for me to pray for myself, or anything else, I am ready to do it, that I may find salvation.

H. I will cheerfully pray for you, if you desire It, or do anything else in my power for you.

S. Thank you, sir; truly I am grateful for your kindness. You no doubt, realize the importance of my pursuing the proper course. I desire, above all things, to proceed according to the will of the Lord. I would not, for worlds, make any mistake where the salvation of my soul is in danger. If, therefore, the Lord requires me to be prayed for, that I may obtain the forgiveness of sins, I desire to do it.

H. I am truly rejoiced, my young friend, to find that you are anxious to seek the Lord. The Savior says, "He who seeks shall find." I trust, then, you will give up your whole heart, and never cease seeking till you find rest to your soul.

S. That is now my intention; but you are aware that I am un-instructed, and do not know where or how to seek the Lord. Knowing, therefore, that you make it your business to teach "those ignorant and out of the way," I have, with the utmost confidence, come to you, to show me what the scriptures require me to do, that I may obtain the forgiveness of sins.

H. I would advise you, my dear young friend, to seek the Lord in prayer. Give up your whole heart to the Lord, and I trust he will have mercy upon you. I would advise you to attend our prayer meetings and the class. These are precious means of grace, through which thousands have been soundly converted to God.

S. Mr. H., I have brought my Bible with me; and, if you please, turn down a leaf at the place where these instructions may be found, that I may read them when alone. I desire to proceed according to Scripture.

H. I did not say that my advice was, in so many words, Scripture; but, after many years' reading and prayerful study, I give it to you as Scriptural advice.

S. Of course there are Scriptures instructing persons, in my condition, how to come to God, from which you deduce this advice. Will you mark some of the places, that I may consider them when in retirement? You know it is important that I should seek according to Scripture. I desire to proceed in such a manner as to enable me to claim the promises of God.

H. Yes, sir; but you need have no fears but you proceed correctly; for prayer is so frequently enjoined in Scripture, that you cannot fail to see that it is right. Besides, the Scriptures say, "Blessed are they who mourn, for they shall be comforted."

S. I have no doubt that prayer is right, for I can recollect of reading of prayer in the Scriptures; but not knowing where to find these passages, and especially where persons seeking the salvation of their souls were commanded to pray, or be prayed for, I desire you to turn down a leaf at a few places. Is the passage you quoted, "Blessed are they who mourn," etc., speaking of conversion?

H. I cannot say it is; but, as you are what we call a "mourner," I thought the language applicable in your case. As to prayer, the Apostle says, "I will, therefore, that men pray everywhere."

S. If that passage speaks of conversion, and is intended for men in my condition, I desire you to mark it here in my Bible. Was it addressed to persons seeking the Lord as I am, or Christians? I am desirous to have the Scripture that relates to my condition.

H. You, my dear young friend, are a seeker, and the Lord says, "I will be sought unto by prayer." Besides, you are a "mourner," in anguish on account of sin. It is right, therefore, that you should seek the Lord in prayer.

S. No doubt you are correct. I have the utmost confidence that you will give me the proper instructions. I have heard of great numbers being converted in olden times, do not know where in the Bible to find the account of these cases. Will you, therefore, refer me to some place where the people came to the "mourner's bench," or the "altar of prayer," to pray and be prayed for? I desire to be certain that I am going according to Scripture.

H. My dear sir, how can you have doubts about prayer, where it is commanded in so many places in Scripture?

S. I have no doubt about it, but I simply desire you to point out some of those places where we read of such great numbers being converted, that I may read for myself where such great numbers were commanded to come to the mourner's bench, or the altar of prayer, to pray and be prayed for. I desire to read these passages, because there are several things about it I do not understand.

H. Perhaps you are unwilling to take my word!

S. Certainly, my dear sir, I am willing to take your word. If you tell me where I can find these passages, I have no doubt I shall find them as you say.

H. You seem to doubt when I tell you that it is your duty to seek the Lord in prayer, that I am right, and, consequently, keep calling for the Scriptures where prayer is required. I am afraid you will not be converted soon, if you continue to manifest such an unwillingness to pray.

S. I trust, sir, you will have patience with me. I am aware that I am ignorant, but you are able to enlighten me. Besides, I have not doubted your veracity at all. I am desirous to pray or do anything the Lord requires. But you must perceive that it is of the utmost importance that, when seeking the salvation of my soul, I should proceed according to the will of the Lord. Now, while I do not doubt that you care and will teach me correctly, and that it is my duty to pray, there are several things in regard to it that I consider indispensible for me to know.

1. I desire to know who is commanded to pray for me.
2. I desire to know whether there is any promise that I shall be heard if I pray for myself.
3. I desire to know how often I should be prayed for, before I have the promise of pardon. It has occurred to me that I may be required to do something else as well as pray, and I am anxious to do my whole duty. Will you, therefore, point out to me those passages where such great numbers are said to have been converted?

H. If you are not willing to use the means of grace which I recommend, and which have proved a. blessing to so many thousand souls, I fear, sir, that I cannot be of any service to you.

S. I am perfectly willing to use any means of grace, and desirous to do so, required in the Scriptures. But I am anxious to use the means of grace according to Scripture. Therefore, I desire you to refer me to those Scriptures which give us an account of so many thousands using the means of grace, that I may proceed as they did.

H. I presume, sir, that you are acquainted with our practice with those who seek salvation; and if you believe in our way, and will go with us, we will do you all the good and give you all the assistance in our power; but if you have no confidence in us, we can do you no good.

S. I have the utmost confidence in you; but you have occasionally exhorted us to read the Scriptures, and I cannot understand why you refuse to refer me to those passages which speak of the conversion of such vast numbers, that I may read for myself where they were commanded to pray and be prayed for, and whatever else they were commanded to do, and do the same. You believe they were converted right, I presume?

H. Certainly they were.

S. Please then, sir, refer me to the passages, as I must now leave, that I may reflect upon them until I see you again.

H. I would advise you to read the Psalms of David, and attend our prayer-meeting on next Thursday night.

S. I will do so. Good bye.

CHAPTER II.

ACCORDING to promise, our young friend, Sincerity, read the Psalms of David through, and, attending the prayer-meeting on Thursday night following the time of the preceding conversation. In the place of the prayer-meeting, (as Mr. Honesty, the Presiding Elder had expected,) he found the church in the midst of a protracted meeting. He said to himself, "I am rejoiced to find such a meeting as this in progress, for I shall have the way to heaven clearly pointed out to me." On entering the church, he was rejoiced to find Mr. H. in the pulpit, reading the following words, "He who seeks shall find." "What precious words to me," said young Sincerity to himself. "I will then seek the Lord with all my heart."

Mr. H. divided his discourse as follows:

1. To show that it is the duty of all to seek.
2. That the way is plain.
3. That the promise is unequivocal—that all who seek shall find.

Upon each of these heads he discoursed as follows:

1. It is the duty of all to seek the Lord. This is sustained by the clear language of Scripture: "He hath made of one blood all nations of men, to dwell on the face of the earth, that they should seek the Lord. If happily they might feel after him and find him, though he be not far from every one of us." Again: "I will be sought unto by prayer." Thus we have shown from God's written word, that all are commanded to seek the Lord.

2. The way is plain. This is proved by the word of the Lord. The prophet says, "The way is so plain, that the wayfaring men, though fools, need not err therein." The gospel was to be a lamp to our path, which shows that the path was to be very plain. Thus you discover the way is plain, so that man is left without excuse.

3. The promise is unequivocal. "To him who asks it shall be given; to him who knocks it shall be opened; he who seeks shall find" And again: "He who cometh to me I will in no wise cast out." "Now is the accepted time: behold, now is the day of salvation." "Whosoever will, let him partake of the water of life freely."

Having now proved from God's written word-

1. That it is the duty of all to seek.
2. That the way is plain.
3. That the promise is unequivocal—that they who seek shall find—the duty of all is manifest.

What, then must the perdition be of those who refuse to seek God! Let me exhort you then, to haste, as for life, to the altar of prayer, and seek God while it is called to-day. Come, now, all things are ready; come, and give us your hand, and we will do you good.

At the conclusion, an invitation was given, and a number of persons rushed to the altar and fell upon their knees. But our young friend, *Sincerity*, kept his seat in the middle of the house, and showed from his countenance, that deep trouble was upon his heart. He sat still, apparently in deep meditation, during some two hours, while the usual exercises of a mourner's bench scene transpired, and, at the close, withdrew in great sadness. As he walked away, he said to himself, "I am afraid this matter of becoming a Christian is a dark subject. The more I think about it, the thicker the gloom. What does it avail to hear a man argue the way is plain, who does not show me this very plain way, I will go to the residence of Mr. Honesty, and have another conversation." In a few moments he raps at the door. "Walk in," responded from within. "Good evening, Mr. S., I am happy to see you, and was greatly rejoiced to see you at our meeting to-night. Have you read the Psalms of David?" said Mr. H.

Sincerity. Yes, sir, and find them extremely interesting, but could not find, as I expected, the way pointed out for me to become a Christian.

Honesty. I labored to point out that to you in my discourse to-night. I hope I have satisfied you in regard to that matter.

S. I am sorry to be compelled to say, Mr. H., that you shed no light on the main difficulty with me. I was satisfied before that it was my duty to seek God, and I had supposed, as you contended, that the way was plain. But from all you have said, I could not see that you pointed out any way to come.

H. Did you not see how those others came?

S. Yes, sir, I saw how they came to the mourner's bench, but I did not see or hear any Scripture, as I had hoped to, requiring them to come in that way. If you had shown the Scripture requiring such procedure, I was ready, at any moment, to have done as they did. But seeing these come as they did, and observing the whole procedure, has involved my mind in such perplexities that I know not what to do.

H. I don't see anything to perplex you, unless it is your own unbelief.

S. It may be unbelief for anything I know, but so it is. I am a miserable being, and hoped that you might relieve me. I cannot rest in this condition.

H. I cannot relieve you unless I know your difficulty. I trust, however, it is the work of conviction you feel, and, if so, I hope it may progress to complete regeneration.

S. My difficulty is this: you argued that it was the sinner's duty to seek; that the way was plain; and that those who seek shall find. A large number came forward seeking, and inquired what they should do to be saved. I anxiously listened to hear you tell them what to do. I heard the directions you gave them, and saw them do what you told them to do in every particular, as it appeared to me, with the deepest anxiety. Am I not right? Did they not seek according to your directions?

H. They did, and I think they did right in so doing. You should have done the same.

S. Well, sir, here is my difficulty: After they had sought according to your directions; had done all you directed, you recollect that you passed along among them, and inquired of them personally, after which you arose and reported that not one of them had got religion! Now, I could not understand this. It was their duty to seek. You said the way was plain, and insisted upon the unequivocal promise, "They who seek shall find." These persons did seek, but, you said, did not find! How is this?

H. Perhaps they may find peace to their souls to-morrow night

S. My dear sir, am I in all this anxiety, and are all these persons, in their deep and intense solicitude, as I saw them tonight to depend on a "perhaps" for the salvation of the soul? If this is where I am to be left, I am in a worse condition then if I had never heard the gospel.

H. My young friend, you are entirely too impatient. I was a seeker six months before the Lord spoke peace to my soul. I have known many to seek for years, and not find peace with God. In some instances I have known persons to join on trial, and seek as high as ten, fifteen and, in some few instances, as high as twenty years, without finding.

S. And yet you tell them the way is plain, and they that seek shall find. Alas! for your plain way, and your Bible promises, if a man may seek fifteen or twenty years and not find!

H. Young man, I see that you have no adequate conception of Christianity.

S. No, sir, I perceive I have not, and what is more mortifying than all, is that I am not likely to have any adequate understanding of the subject; for nothing but clouds of gloom and darkness rise before me. Am I to have no Scripture directions to guide me? Is there no way laid down in the Bible, by which I may come to the Lord?

H. I do not say that you must seek as great a length of time as some I have mentioned—many get through much sooner. You may get through in a week, two weeks, or six months. You might get religion the first time you came to the mourner's bench. You should not despair, nor become impatient.

S. But, my dear sir, if the way is so plain, as you have represented, and we have the promise that they who seek shall find how is it that you suspend the whole matter in doubt, saying, "I may get religion," on the first application, the second, etc? Is there no definite place where I can come to the unequivocal promise of God?

H. I have already shown you the promise; and, if you have any faith, you cannot doubt the Lord's promise; but you must wait for the Lord's own good time.

S. Does not the Scripture say, "Now is the accepted time, and now is the day of salvation," some place? Does it not say "To-day, if you will hear his voice," etc? Did not many thousands anciently come to the Lord in a single day?

H. There are such passages as you refer to, and many did come, and obtain peace with God in a single day in olden times, but it is not so now.

S. Why is it not so now? Who has changed the order?

H. Times have changed. The Scripture says—, I—I—If you desire to go with us, we will do all for you we can; but, with your notions, I can do but little for you.

S. I have no notions, know nothing about what is right. but wish you would show me how so many turned to the Lord in a day. Good night.

CHAPTER III.

AFTER the conversation with Mr. H., in the previous chapter, our young friend, Sincerity, retired to his sleeping apartment, but not to sleep. He laid himself upon his bed and soliloquized as follows:

"I see that I am awfully deluded. I had supposed it was a very plain matter to become a Christian, and, therefore, indifferently put off this important work, till, in all probability, a majority of my days are numbered. I am perfectly astonished and overwhelmed to find that now I am anxious to seek the salvation of my soul, the whole matter appears involved in obscurity. Is it possible that the salvation of the world is wrapped up in so much mystery and obscurity as this? Is it possible that a learned ministry, called and sent of God to preach the gospel, can throw no clearer light upon the subject than my friend, Mr. H., has given me? I supposed, when he advised me to read the Psalms of David, that I should there find the account of the conversion of those vast multitudes of whom I had heard the preachers speak so frequently, and how they were converted, but, to my utter astonishment, I found nothing in regard to these matters, nor anything showing how I might become a disciple of Christ. I am equally astonished, that now I am resolved to read the Bible through, and have read the five books of Moses, I have been unable to find anything relating directly to myself, or showing me the way to heaven. I found these ancient records filled with matters of great interest; but how am I to know the way to heaven from these lengthy records of antiquity?

"I am perfectly confounded, and know not what to do. It is certainly true that I am a sinner, and must be lost if I am not pardoned. I am equally certain that Christ is the Lord and Redeemer of men; and that he invites all to come to him is equally true. Why is it, then, that no way is pointed out by which to come? Would the Lord invite men to come to him, knowing that they would be lost if they did not come, and yet point out no way to come? He certainly would not. He could not do this, and then declare the way so plain that "the wayfaring men, though simpletons, need not err therein," nor could he, if no way is pointed out, say that "he who seeks shall find." Why is it, then, that I cannot find the way? I certainly could see the way if it had been pointed out to me. I certainly desire to find the way and know the truth. I cannot say, then, why I should be left in this state of despondency.

"I cannot understand Mr. H. He has always appeared to me to be a good man, and I have tried to treat him kindly. Yet he appeared to speak once or twice in our conversation, as though he thought I was uncandid. I cannot see why he should be unwilling to refer me to the passages that speak of mourners coming forward to pray and be prayed for. I recollect that he would not refer me to the place where I could find an account of the conversion of such vast multitudes. It appeared to me rational, as I desired to come to the Lord, to read the account of such vast numbers coming, and see for myself how they came. Why, then, did he evade, and fail to point out to me these passages? He certainly knew where they were. I cannot understand this."

Such were the meditations of *Sincerity*, after his retirement. Early in the morning, Mr. H. rapped at his door. "Good morning," said Mr. H., "how do you do this morning?"

S. My general health is good, but I could not rest last night. I am in much anxiety and greatly confounded in regard to my salvation. I was surprised, and confounded, Mr. H., when you failed to point out to me, from the Scriptures, how I should come to the Lord. Can you, my dear sir, give me the source to which I am to apply for the evidence of pardon?

H. You must have the evidence of pardon within.

S. How am I to know that it is within

H. You must feel that your sins are forgiven.

S. What kind of feelings must I have, as an evidence of the pardon of sin?

H. Good feelings—joyful feelings, as a matter of course. You must feel that your load of guilt is gone, and that the Lord has spoken peace to your soul.

S. And that is the evidence of pardon!

H. Yes, sir. When the Lord converted my soul, it appeared to me that a mountain had been taken off of me. It appeared to me that all nature changed, and that all the trees, the green fields, the fowls of heaven, and the fish of the sea—that everything in heaven and upon earth, praised God, and I was enabled to say, "I know that my Redeemer lives," and that "Jesus has power on earth to forgive sins." This, sir, is the evidence of pardon—the witness in myself that I am a child of God.

S. What is the cause of your rejoicing?

H. Because I have got religion, thank God!

S. What is the evidence that you have got religion?

H. My joyful feelings.

S. Is that the way the matter stands in the Bible?

H. My young friend, I am afraid you are skeptical. It appears to me that you are inclined to doubts. I would advise you to pray that you may be delivered from unbelief. The religion I have, of course, is Scriptural.

S. I may be skeptical, but I do not think I am. At all events, I desire to believe, and desire to be a Christian. But I cannot see how you make my inquiry, whether you make feeling the result of religion, or religion the result of feeling, an indication that I am skeptical. I simply desire to know whether feeling is the Scriptural evidence of pardon.

H. My dear young friend, I must say to you candidly, that I have, from our first conversation, feared that you are skeptical, but shall be happy to find that you are not. But that feeling is the evidence of pardon, is manifested both from Scripture and reason. Seek the Lord, that you may find the salvation of your soul, and feel the power of pardoning love. I must see those persons who came to the mourner's bench last night, and see if they have found peace with God. Come to meeting tonight. Good-by.

While *Sincerity* was reflecting on this conversation, a Romanist came in, to whom he said, "Where do you find Scripture to prove that the priest can forgive sins?"

Romanist. I do not ask for Scripture to prove that the priest can forgive sins; I know that the priest can forgive sins.

Sincerity. How do you know it?

R. How do I know that the priest can forgive sins? Why, or, when I am laded and pressed down with my numerous sins, I go to the priest and humbly confess—unbosom my whole soul to him, and the holy father forgives me. I know that I am pardoned, because I feel that the great burden—my oppressive load of guilt—is gone. I feel that I am delivered, and return to my home happy.

S. But where is the Scripture for that?

R. What need have I for Scripture? Don't I know when I am pardoned, when I feel that my load of sin and guilt is gone?

After the Romanist had gone, our young friend said to himself: "Is it possible that Romanists have the same evidence of pardon as other people. I am unable to understand how this is. If feeling is the evidence of pardon for anything I can see to the contrary, this Romanist has proved that a priest can pardon him, just as Mr. H. proved that the Lord pardoned him. Am I to have no evidence of pardon only such as a Romanist may have, to prove that a priest can pardon him? Have Protestants no higher evidence of pardon than Romanists? This involves me in a worse confusion than ever! Am I blinded by unbelief, as Mr. H. seems to think, or what is the matter? I am perfectly astonished at the condition of religious matters. My confusion becomes worse and worse, the more I think upon the subject.

Our young friend passed along up the street, and heard a man preaching in an old, dilapidated house, with some three small windows, and he seated himself in the house. It turned out to be an Anti-Means Baptist, preaching upon the words, "Whom He will, He hardeneth," to an audience of about fifteen persons, several of whom were soundly asleep. He was pretty much through his discourse when *Sincerity* entered. But in summing up his discourse, he insisted, "that God passed by the non-elect, made no provision for them; that Christ did not die for them; that the Lord hardened them; blinded them, sent them strong delusions that they could not, in any event, turn to God, or be saved."

Sincerity walked away saying to himself, "Perhaps I am one of the non-elect, and blinded. I cannot think that I am hardened, or that I am given over to believe a lie. If I know my own heart, I desire to know and believe the truth. I thought preachers were designed to enlighten the world; but if they are, I cannot understand them. I fear that I am lost!"

CHAPTER IV.

As our young friend returned home, after hearing the Calvinist Baptist, he met with a Universalist preacher, in conversation with a lawyer of his acquaintance, a skeptic; when the following conversation took place:

Lawyer. Mr. S., what is the matter that you are following the preachers up? Are you about being deluded by the noise and pretenses of religion?

Sincerity. I am greatly distressed in regard to my salvation. I had supposed that religion was a very plain matter, and that one could become a Christian at any time; but the more I think about it, the greater my perplexity.

L. Yes, sir; and the more you try to understand it, the more you will be perplexed. In my younger days, I was in the same condition with yourself. I listened to the preachers several years, but found that I could not understand them, that they disagree among themselves and, having turned my attention to the law, I have found something tangible, and that can be acted upon, and have, therefore, concluded to leave my salvation to God. I will try and look out for myself in this world, and leave God to take care of me in the next, if there be any.

S. I am inclined to think—indeed, I am compelled to admit —that so far as my experience goes, what you say about the preachers, appears to be the case. But then they are good men certainly.

L. I admit, freely, that they are good men. Here is our neighbor, H., the Presiding Elder; he is a good, and self-sacrificing man. He spends his whole time in preaching, and visiting the members of his church, and, I think, only receives some "three hundred dollars a year for his services, while I make a thousand a year with far less labor. Yet I have listened to him trying to point out the way of salvation, and I could see no plan or system that any man of sense could act upon, or, in other words, I could see nothing tangible that I could take hold of. Not only so, but I have seen numbers of sincere persons come to him in the church, and inquire of him what to do, and have heard him tell them to pray and be prayed for, and have seen him pray for them, and they would still go away mourning and lamenting that they were not pardoned."

S. I have seen the same, and have had several private conversations with Mr. H., in which he failed to give me any satisfaction in regard to the way of salvation; and as you say, it does appear to me that he had no plan. I think that, though he is a good, an honest, and a sincere man, he does not understand the gospel.

L. No, Mr. S., you do not apprehend the difficulty. He is, as you say, a good, an honest and sincere man, but he is deluded, and the preachers are all in the same predicament. None of them understand; and the reason is, religion is all a delusion; it has no understanding to it.

S. If I thought all the preachers were as incapable of giving light as Mr. H., I should be even more miserable than I am. But it is mortifying and discouraging to me to hear you ascribe the blame to religion itself. My impression is that the fault is in incompetency of some men to set forth Christianity, and not in the obscurity in religion itself.

L. There is where you are mistaken; the fault is not in the men, but in religion. If you desire to obtain relief from your despondency, you had better drive this gloomy subject from your mind. Turn your attention to your business, and try to take care of yourself, for if you do not take care of yourself, nobody will do it for you. Come over the way, and let us get something to take, and not allow ourselves to fall into gloomy despondency

Universalist. Mr. L., I think you have passed but a poor compliment upon religion and ministers. If you will allow me to explain to you the blessed gospel of God's universal paternity, I can show you how you can find comfort to your mind, and how our mutual friend, Sincerity, may find relief from all his troubles. I see what it is, Mr. L., that has driven you, and will drive you, Mr. S., into unbelief, if you are not relieved. It is the Pagan notion of "everlasting punishment"—"eternal damnation." If you once understood the blessed doctrine of a world's salvation, your mind would be at rest.

S. Your idea is then, if I understand you, that the source of my distress is in a misapprehension of mind, and not in any real danger.

U. I think, sir, that you are actually in a dangerous condition, but the danger is not what you fear. The only thing that will afford you relief is the blessed doctrine of a world's salvation.

S. You consider, then, that I am really safe if I only knew it, and all that is necessary is to show me and your friend here

Mr. L., that we are in no danger, to make us happy.

U. Yes, sir, that is, there is no danger of any "eternal damnation," or "everlasting punishment," as the orthodox teach.

L. Did you say, sir, that the orthodox doctrine of "eternal damnation" and "everlasting punishment," is a "Pagan notion?"

U. Yes, sir, I did, and can prove it.

L. Well, then, sir, Jesus taught -Pagan notions," for he used this identical language. He spoke of persons whom he declared to be in danger of "eternal damnation," and others whom he declared should go into "everlasting punishment." This is the teaching of your master, and this you call "Pagan notions." Is this the respect you show to the teachings of Jesus?

U. These passages do not mean that—the fact is-

L. The fact is, you do not believe your Bible any more than I do, nor do you any more honor Jesus. He says, "He who believeth not the Son, shall not see life.". Do you believe this?

U. That passage means—I—I—I—can prove that all shall see life, and-

L. And, as a matter of course, that your Master did not tell the truth when he said, "He that believeth not the Son shall not see life." How is this?

U. I can prove—I can show—the Bible says-

L. The Bible says that you "strengthen the hands of the wicked that he should not return from his wicked way promising him life.". Still you will dishonor the Bible in promising the wicked life, and strengthen the hands of the wicked that he should not return from his wicked way, will you?

U. That means—I hold—I—I—if I talk any more it shall be with a man who has some sense, and not with you, sir. Good-by.

L. You may have some sense, but there is no sense in your doctrine. Friend *Sincerity*, let me say to you, before we separate, that this kind of treatment from preachers has convinced me that religion is all a delusion. None of their doctrine Is true. As I said before, I shall try and take care of myself in this world, and trust to God to take care of me hereafter. I must go. Good-by.

Sincerity walked along homeward, ruminating in his mind as follows: "My trouble increases upon me every day. In the place of finding any relief, new difficulties rise before me. These unfortunate men with whom I have been conversing have not one ray of light. If there is nothing better than they can present, the world is lost. Is it possible that people in general have no better understanding in regard to these matters than those with whom I have conversed? I am perfectly confounded! Can it be that Mr. L. is right, and that religion is all a delusion? I hope he is not, for then all must be darkness and gloom. In this case we must live in uncertainty and die in doubt. The thought of giving up all hope of finding any better instruction is unsupportable. I can not endure it. I will go home and read my Bible through, at all events. I am wretched now, and certainly should be miserable to die in this condition. I have now found four classes of men, and neither of them have afforded me the least satisfaction."

1. Mr. H. insists upon the necessity of seeking the Lord. In this he has satisfied me that he is right; but he has shown me no directions from the Bible, pointing me the way to the Lord.

2. The Calvinist Baptist insists that I can do nothing, and that if I am of the non-elect I can never come to the Lord, matter how I seek. This I do not believe, for the Lord would not require me to seek him, knowing that I could do nothing.

3. My neighbor, the lawyer, has become disgusted with the whole matter, and has resolved to engross his mind with the affairs of the world, and leave the result with God, believing that religion is all a delusion.

4. As to this Universalist preacher, he is trying to satisfy his own mind, and the minds of others, with the notion that man is safe without any conversion, for there is no danger of being lost, as there is no hell or lake of fire. But this most ridiculous, absurd and blasphemous doctrine gives the lie to the whole Bible, for its whole spirit is, "except ye repent, ye shall perish."

In my opinion these latter three doctrines, if they are doctrines, are useless, as neither proposes to make the world any better, or do anything for the world. I could see propriety in the position of Mr. H. if he could show me what the Scriptures require me to do. But I must read my Bible through, and see if I can find something better.

CHAPTER V.

OUR young friend was passing up Clinton Street, Cincinnati, between Western Row and John street, and he saw a Methodist minister, accompanied by some ten or a dozen persons, entering the basement of the chapel belonging to the "Christians," or "Disciples of Christ," as they call themselves, their regular preacher being present. Here a new subject presented itself to the consideration of young Sincerity.. The little company approached the Baptistery, the lids of which were folded back out of the way, and all eyes were directed down into an emblematical tomb, some ten feet in length and four feet wide. The water was some two and a half or three feet in depth. All stood in profound silence, with their eyes fixed upon the solemn looking place. Presently the Methodist minister, and two respectable ladies, all dressed in black, with countenances solemn as the grave, made their appearance near this lowly tomb, where the minister made the following address:

> "Dearly beloved, forasmuch as all men are conceived and born in sin (and that which is born of the flesh is flesh; and they that are in the flesh can not please God, but live in sin, committing many actual transgressions:), and that our Saviour, Christ, saith, None can enter into the kingdom of God except he be regenerated, and born anew of water and the Holy Ghost, and received into

Christ's holy church, and be made lively members of the same."—Dis., p. 107.

The minister then made the following prayer:

"Almighty and immortal God, the aid of all that need, the helper of all that flee to thee for succor, the life of them that believe, and the resurrection of the dead, we call upon thee for these persons, that they, coming to thy holy baptism, may receive remission of their sins, by spiritual regeneration. Receive them, Lord, as thou hast promised by thy well-beloved Son, saying, Ask, and you shall receive; seek, and ye shall find, knock, and it shall be opened unto you; so give now unto us that ask, let us that seek find, open the gate unto us that knock, that these persons may enjoy the everlasting benediction of thy heavenly washing, and may come to the eternal kingdom which thou hast promised by Christ our Lord. Amen."—Dia., p. 107.

He then descended, with one of the ladies, into the baptismal water, and, lifting his eyes and hand toward heaven, uttered in a strong, clear and solemn voice, the following most fearful and awful of all the formulas ever uttered by human lips: "I baptize you into the name of the Father, and of the Son, and of the Holy Ghost. Amen." As he uttered this profoundly awful sentence, with the little company standing around, and breathing almost suspended, he lowered the candidate gently down, till the waters closed above, thus separating her from the visible world. In the next moment she appeared again, as the waters parted from above her in the form of a resurrection from the dead, and an actual resurrection to a new life, and she was joyfully received by those standing by. The other lady passed through the same sacred ceremony. The minister then ascended the steps, or, as the Scripture expresses it, "came up out of the water," and, lifting his hands and eyes toward heaven, said, "May grace, mercy and peace, from God, the Father, and our Lord Jesus Christ, be with us all—now, henceforth and forever mere. Amen."

The minister walked away, apparently conscious of having done his duty. Sincerity stood by trembling, and the tears imperceptibly trickling down his manly cheeks. As he walked away he said to himself: "I thought Methodists did not believe in immersion! But this man seemed sincere in what he did— how is this? Besides, I have never witnessed any religious ceremonies that produced such an effect upon my own sensibilities as this. Possibly it is my duty to be baptized! I certainly should delight to do so if I understood the matter and thought myself prepared. I will see my friend, Mr. H., once more, and have a conversation with him on baptism."

In a few moments he was in the studio of Mr. H., when the following conversation took place:

H. Well, Mr. S., have you become any better reconciled in your mind?

S. No, sir; I am as much perplexed and confused as I have been at any former period. I have had several conversations, and heard some preaching since I saw you, but all without affording me the least relief. Did you know of the baptizing by the Methodist preacher in charge on — Street, in the baptistery of the "Campbellite" Church, on Clinton Street, this morning?

H. Yes, sir; I know all about it. Were you present?

S. Yes, sir; it was a solemn and interesting scene.

H. The facts in the case are these: There were quite a number who joined our church, as you are aware, and, as our Discipline requires all to be baptized before they are received into full fellowship, it devolved upon myself to preach a sermon on baptism. This I did, and satisfied all, except the two you saw dipped this morning, that sprinkling would do, and administered the ordinance to them in that way. But nothing would do these two but that they must be dipped; and, as my health Is delicate, I can not endure the least exposure to wet without imminent danger of violent cold, probably terminating in consumption, I would not consent to go into the water, at such a time as this to gratify the weakness of anybody. The truth is, baptism is not a saving ordinance anyhow.

S. I am surprised to hear you say that, for your preaching brother told us this morning that our Saviour says that "None can enter the kingdom of God except he be regenerated, and born anew of water and the Holy Ghost," and exhorted those present to call upon God to "Grant the persons to be baptized that which by nature they can not have." He also prayed that they might receive remission of their sins, and that the Lord would receive them, from which, I thought, he regarded it as a saving ordinance.

H. You must have misunderstood him—he did not mean that.

S. But he had your book of Discipline in his hand, and understood him to be uttering the precise words of the Discipline.

H. You do not understand this matter. We do not believe that baptism is essential.

S. Is it true, as your preaching brother said this morning, that our Saviour says that "None can enter the kingdom of God except he be born of water and the Holy Ghost"

H. Certainly it is; it is so stated in our discipline.

S. How can any be saved without it, then? If none can enter the kingdom of God without being "born of water and the Holy Ghost"— and being born of water is baptism, as you admit your Discipline implies—how can any be saved without it? Can they be saved without entering into the kingdom of God?

H. None can enter—none can enter—the kingdom of God there means—the fact is, the mode is not revealed.

S. Am I to understand you that the manner in which baptism is to be administered is not revealed?

H. Yes, sir; no man can show from the Bible that any mode is revealed.

S. If it is not revealed how a thing is to be done, how is a person to know how to do it? or how can any living man know whether it is done at all or not?

H. I regard it as valid when performed either way, by sprinkling, pouring or immersion.

S. But, my dear sir, if the manner of obeying the command to be baptized is not revealed, it is wholly in the dark, and there is no evidence that either sprinkling, pouring or immersion is baptism.

H. I can prove sprinkling from Scripture. It says, "I will sprinkle many nations."

S. I thought you said the mode is not revealed! If It is not revealed, how can you prove it to be sprinkling?

H. I am, sir, afraid your condition is lamentable. I fear you will turn into skepticism. You produce nothing but difficulties. The mode of baptism is plainly taught in the baptism of the Holy Ghost. The Lord said, "I will pour out my spirit." This proves that pouring is the mode.

S. Mr. H., I hope I shall not become a skeptic; but, if I can not find something more consistent, and that I can understand better than what you have taught. I do not know where I shall land. You first tell me, of baptism, that no mode is revealed: then, in the next moment, you are trying to prove that sprinkling is baptism. Then, again, you are trying to prove pouring. In the place of no mode being revealed, you would have me believe that two or three modes are revealed?

As our young friend walked away he said to himself: "Is this the way ministers are enlightening the world? Is there nothing in religion that I can understand? If there is no clearer light than this I am a miserable man!"

CHAPTER VI.

Our young friend, *Sincerity*, shortly after his late conversation with Mr. H., was at a funeral, and, being detained by the failure of the undertaker to arrive in time, his attention was attracted by the conversation of a very grave, dignified and thoughtful lady, in appearance, who sat near him, and directed her discourse to some ladies at her side. He soon found that her remarks were of a religious character, and of course was deeply interested in them. But he could not discover what religious party this venerable lady was of; yet he was struck with the sense and propriety of what she said. For the present we shall call this distinguished and interesting lady Priscilla. When the conversation had terminated between her and those to whom she directed her remarks our young friend approached her as follows:

Sincerity. May I ask, madam, to what denomination you belong

Priscilla. The Church of Christ, sir.

S. I supposed you belonged to the Church of Christ; but what branch?

P. I do not belong to a branch, my good sir, but am a branch myself. The Saviour said to his disciples, "I am the Vine, ye are the branches."

I trust, sir, that I am one of these branches, or a member of Christ's body—the church.

S. Well, but what do you and your brethren call yourselves?

P. Christians, sir; Disciples of Christ.

S. Nothing else?

P. Sometimes we call the members of the church "brethren," "friends," "children of God," "saints," etc., as they did in ancient times. We apply to ourselves none but Scriptural designations.

S. Why, I am astonished! How do you distinguish yourselves from others?

P. We do not wish to distinguish ourselves from others who are satisfied with the simple designations or which the people of God are called in the Scriptures. But those who are not satisfied with Scripture designations for the children of God, by calling themselves by other names, distinguish themselves from us. There is, therefore, a distinction kept up where there Is a difference, and that is as far as there should be any distinction.

S. Well, this is a new idea to me. You say you simply apply to yourselves Scripture names, as you find them in the Bible?

P. No, sir, not exactly as we find them in the Bible, as we find them in the New Testament. We are not Jews, but Christians; not under Moses, but Jesus; not under the law, but the gospel; not under the letter, but the Spirit.

R. If I understand, then, you call yourselves Christians, Disciples, etc., as the followers of Christ did in New Testament times, and nothing else. Am I right?

P. Yes, sir. Is that not sufficient? If you were about to die, and knew yourself to be a Christian, a Disciple of Christ, etc., would you not be satisfied?

S. I must confess that I would. That is precisely what I have been desiring to know and inquiring into for weeks. What doctrine do you hold, madam?

P. The doctrine of Christ, of Christianity.

S. Nothing else

P. No, sir, nothing else. The Lord has given nothing else. We need nothing else. Not only so, but the Lord has pronounced a curse upon man or angel who shall preach anything else, or even pervert the gospel of Christ. Are you not satisfied to receive Christianity—pure and unadulterated Christianity, as the Lord gave it, and nothing else?

S. Yes, if I knew how to receive Christianity as God gave it, and nothing else, and how to become a Christian, or a disciple of Christ, as you seem to think one may, it would be a relief to me worth more than worlds but this is where my trouble lies. I have had several conversations with Mr. H., but find it utterly impossible for me to understand him. He thinks I am blinded by unbelief. I confess I am blinded by some means; I do not understand.

P. My dear sir, I have not an unkind feeling toward Mr. H., or a hard word to say of him. He is evidently a kind-hearted man, and is just about sufficiently enlightened as to conduct a mourner's bench excitement, without Scripture or understanding but he is as ignorant as a new-born infant of the Bible plan of salvation, and what is worse in his case than that of an infant, he is so blinded by bigotry, sectarian partisan zeal and self-conceit that there is even less hope of his ever being enlightened than an infant. The reason you could not understand him was that he presented nothing tangible that your mind could take hold of.

S. That is what my friend, the lawyer, told me in a conversation the other day, but he said the fault was in religion— that there is no understanding in it.

P. I am acquainted with your friend, the gentleman of the legal profession, and consider him an honorable man of the world, but he has been confused with sectarian difficulties and absurdities, and is now a skeptic. But this want of intelligibility is not in religion itself, but in the confused minds of men, who have never learned to take hold of religion at its beginning.

S. Madam, will you tell me what its beginning is?

P. Its beginning and ending is the Lord Jesus Christ, the Saviour of the world. He is revealed to the unconverted and unbelieving world in the four gospels, Matthew, Mark, Luke and John. Hence John says, "These things are written that you might believe." When the inquirer has examined these divine testimonies concerning Christ, and believes on Him as a divine person, the Saviour and Redeemer, it leads him to inquire what he shall do to be saved.

S. Allow me to say, madam, that that is precisely where I am now standing. I believe in the Saviour with all my heart, and love Him, but can not find how I am to come to Him.

P. You are then prepared to proceed to the second division of the New Testament, the Acts of Apostles, and read the inspired accounts of the numerous cases of conversions there recorded, that you may proceed in the same way they did, to obtain pardon and admission into the kingdom of God.

S. That is precisely the part of the Bible I desired to find, but Mr. H. evaded and did not point it out to me. I was at the protracted meeting held by Mr. H., and saw a number of persons come forward to pray and be prayed for, and requested him to point out to me where the Scriptures mention such vast numbers turning to the Lord, that I might read for myself, and learn precisely what they were required to do; but, for some cause, he did not point out the place to me. Did you say I would find this in the Acts of the Apostles?

P. Yes, sir; you will there find the account of all the conversions recorded in the Scriptures. But you will find nothing there, or any place in the Bible, about coming to the mourner's bench to pray and be prayed for. There was no such procedure in the Apostles' times.

S. What, then, were they required to do?

P. You will find, Acts ii. 38, where a vast number inquired what they should do, and where the inspired Apostles answered them. Read the case for yourself and the whole book of Acts through, against I see you again, and you can tell yourself what they required to do as well as any preacher in the city.

CHAPTER VII.

OUR young friend, *Sincerity*, after his conversation at the funeral with *Mrs. Priscilla*, returned to his room, and read the Acts of the Apostles through once every day for a week. Just as he had closed his seventh reading the Presiding Elder, Mr. H., rapped at his door, and was soon seated with our young friend by his pleasant fire. After the usual compliments, the following conversation ensued:

H. Have you become any better reconciled in your mind in regard to the salvation of your soul?

S. Yes, sir; I have had a conversation with Mrs. Priscilla, and-

H. And she is about to make a Campbellite of you, Is she?

S. No, sir; she said nothing about making a Campbellite, or any other kind of an ite; but she gave me more satisfaction about becoming a Christian than all the other instructors I have had.

H. I know her; she knows nothing about religion; she is a woman I can not endure. Did she tell you that you would have to be dipped or you could not be saved?

S. No, sir; she said nothing about being "dipped," as you call it.

H. Well, that is surprising; she generally makes immersion the great essential, and contends that unless persons are immersed they can not be saved.

S. She did not mention immersion to me; and I think you are entirely too hasty thus to prejudge her.

U. I have no patience with such women. It is ridiculous for them to sit up and discuss doctrinal matters.

S. I never saw the lady before, but, she appeared unassuming, and certainly showed an intimate acquaintance with the Scriptures.

H. I have seen such folks before, and found that, though they showed an intimate acquaintance with the Scriptures, they knew nothing about religion.

S. Do not the Scriptures treat of religion"? and if they do, how can a person have an intimate acquaintance with them and know nothing about religion?

H. A person may understand the Scriptures—a person may know—the truth is—what did Mrs. Priscilla say that afforded you so much satisfaction?

S. I cannot now repeat over all she said, but the main Item from which I have derived satisfaction was the simple direction, where in the Bible I could find an account of conversions, and how sinners were converted.

H. She told you to read the second chapter of Acts, I will vouch for; did she not?

S. She told me to read the whole of Acts through, and see for myself what the Apostles preached, and-

H. I know her deception; do not let her deceive you with any of her novel notions.

S. It cannot be possible that she was trying to deceive me, unless

the Bible itself will deceive, for she showed me where to read and learn for myself. She claimed to be nothing but a Christian, to belong to no church but the Church of Christ, and did not attempt to explain to me, but advised me to read for myself.

H. All that is quite specious; it is plausible enough, and well calculated to deceive the unsuspecting. But she did not come out fully. I have heard her preacher deliver some discourses that were exceptionable, but it was at times when he did not come out fully.

S. Well, sir, I can not see how there can be any deception in her course. She instructed me to read the sermons of the Apostles, believe what they preached, precisely as those to whom they preached did; and when I came to where persons inquired what they must do to be saved, under the preaching of the Apostles, I must notice what they were directed to do, how they did it, and do the same for the same purpose.

H. I say, sir, it is all deception, and its great plausibility is calculated to delude and ruin men, and-

S. There is Mrs. Priscilla now, passing through the hall; I will invite her in, and have you explain this matter. Mrs. Priscilla, please walk in. My friend, Mr. H., has given me a friendly call, and I have been relating our conversation to him, and wish to hear him and yourself converse upon the subject of our conversation at the funeral the other day.

H. Madame, you are aware that I am no friend to controversy,

P. I presume so, sir, and I do not set myself up as competent to discuss doctrinal points with a gentleman who has made religion the study of his life.

S. I was telling my friend, Mr. H., of your recommendation for me to read the Acts of Apostles through, which I have done seven times over since I saw you, with great satisfaction. But he thinks your instructions are deceptive.

P. Mr. H., do you not believe that the same doctrine the Apostles preached should be preached now?

H. Undoubtedly it should.

P. Should it not have the same effect,

H. Most assuredly it should.

P. Where the same doctrine is preached, and the same effect is produced, will not people now, as they did then, cry out "Men and brethren, what shall we do?"

H. Most certainly, and many have cried out the same way during our great revival.

P. Should not the same answer given in such cases by the Apostles be given now to inquirers?

H. They should be answered—I should tell them—the Scripture says—the fact is, I am not bound to answer your question.

P. No, sir, but you are bound, as a gentleman, but more especially as a Christian, if you allege that I am a deceiver, to show wherein. You have granted that what the Apostles preached should be preached now; that what the first converts believed should be believed now; that it should have the same effect upon the heart now it did then, inducing the people to cry out, "Men and brethren, what shall we do?" But when I ask you if the same answer should not be given to the inquiry now as given to it then, you say you are not bound to answer, but still allege that I am a deceiver. Am I deceiving when I insist on following the exact teachings of the Apostles?

H. I do not mean that you designedly deceive.

P. How can I be deceiving at all, either intentionally or unintentionally, when I insist on believing all the Apostles preached, doing exactly what, they commanded. for the same purpose, that precisely the same effect may be produced, and that the subject may have the same enjoyments? I simply desire everything as God gave it, nothing more, nothing less. Is this deceiving?

H. Madam, I can not subscribe to your views; they are disastrous to vital piety.

P. I did not ask you to subscribe to my views, but desire you to show how it could deceive any person to be directed to the first teachings and practice of the Apostles after the Lord ascended to heaven, to learn how persons were converted, and insist on their being converted in the same way now. Do you believe those converted on the day of Pentecost were converted right?

H. I believe—I hold—the Scriptures say, "Let every man be fully persuaded in his own mind."

P. That is, if one man is persuaded to be a Mormon, another a Universalist, another a Romanist, etc., it is all right, is it?

H. Madam, you have a peculiar method of turning everything your own way. That passage, you must know, can have no such signification as that.

P. No, sir, nor does it have any such signification as you have given it, nor has it any reference to the conversion of sinners, but it has reference to things pertaining to our practice, wherein we are entirely free, or where there is no law binding in any way, as in reference to eating meat, where we are left entirely free to eat or not, as we may be persuaded in our own minds. But, sir, did Peter answer the three thousand on the day of Pentecost rightly, when they cried out, "What shall we do?"

H. Mrs. P., why do you ask that question? You know that we do not hold alike, and you can have your own opinion and allow me to have mine.

P. It is not a question of opinion, or whether we hold alike; but did the inspired Apostle answer rightly?

H. I tell you, madam, we can not see alike.

S. Mrs. P., I have read the Acts of the Apostles through seven times since I saw you, and am satisfied that Peter answered correctly on the day of Pentecost, for he "preached the gospel with the Holy Ghost sent down from heaven, which things the angels desire to look into." I have been for weeks making inquiry what I should do to be saved; but I now believe all the Apostles preached, and am determined to do what they commanded.

H. I saw from the beginning that you would have your own way. Good-bye.

S. I intended to have the Lord's way, if it was to be found, and, having now found It, I am determined to walk in it.

CHAPTER VIII.

A SHORT time after the foregoing interview Sincerity called to have another conversation with Mrs. Priscilla, which resulted in the following:

Sincerity. I understood you to say that in the Acts of the Apostles we have the only historical accounts of conversions to Christianity found in the whole Bible. Am I right?

Priscilla. You are right, when the statement is properly qualified. The Acts of the Apostles contains all the accounts of conversions to Christianity after the Christian institution was complete, and the full gospel, in fact, was preached.

S. Let me interrupt you. What do you mean by the gospel being preached "in fact?"

P. I find a distinction made in the Bible between the gospel preached in promise and the gospel preached in fact. The gospel may be preached in promise and be believed in promises, without being understood. Paul says, Gal. iii. 8, "The gospel was preached to Abraham, saying, In thee and thy seed shall all nations be blessed." This was the whole gospel, concentrated in a promise—the promise that God made to Abraham. But Paul defines the gospel, 1 Cor. xv. 3, to be "that Christ died for our sins according to the Scriptures." The language is of the Almighty to Abraham is a promise. The death of Christ is the accomplishment of that promise in fact. The gospel in promise is the promise of Christ, and the gospel in him, many centuries before he came, but the gospel in fact is the death of Christ according to the Scriptures, and the full gospel developed through him, as Paul expresses it, "made manifest among all nations for the obedience of faith." In other words, the promise to Abraham preached the gospel prospectively, or as something good to come; but the Apostles, after the resurrection of Christ, preached it in fact, or as something good that had come.

All the good things which God had in store for the ages to come, or all included in the new institution, were embraced in the promise to Abraham, but hid from the world—even from the wise and prudent, and revealed to babes—the Apostles, that they might preach to the nations the unsearchable riches of Christ. The whole history of the Bible—the dealings of God with the patriarchs, with the prophets, with the seed of Abraham, with all nations, and all promises, are clearly seen to be from the one same omniscient Ruler of the universe, all tending toward and pointing to the one great fact—the death of Christ. All the prophecies, all the promises, and all the revelations of God to man, concentrate upon the person of Christ. His death for our sins, his burial and resurrection from the dead, according to the Scriptures, for our justification, may be regarded as the center of the whole spiritual system. God has now exalted him to heaven, and demands the attention of the world to him, declaring that to him every knee shall bow and every tongue confess.

S. Allow me again to interrupt you in your interesting remarks. I am delighted with Christianity; it honors our Saviour. But I am surprised on reading the Acts of the Apostles to find that they did not explain their views to their converts before baptizing them, nor do I find where any related their experiences or gave their views of the gospel.

P. I was going to set that matter forth when you stopped me. As Christ and all Christianity were included in the promise to Abraham, so Christ and all Christianity are included in the fact that he died for our sins, according to the Scriptures. Therefore, he who anciently received the promise received Christ; so he now who receives the fact receives Christ and all that is contained in him. The Old Testament and the New center in him. God is in him. Heaven is in him. All the blessings that God bestows upon his children in this world are in him. The whole Christian revelation concentrates itself in him.

S. I can now see what is meant by "preaching Christ," as mentioned in Scripture. It includes all that he authorizes.

P. Precisely so;. and, on the other hand, when Paul determined to "know nothing but Christ, and him crucified," he determined to know nothing except what Christ authorizes. Hence receiving Christ is receiving all that he teaches, and rejecting him is rejecting all his teachings.

S. In that view of the subject, I can see how people were converted immediately on hearing the gospel. They did not wait to understand the whole system, but simply received the Author of it, being assured that he was a divine person, and could teach nothing wrong.

P. Yes, sir; and, having such love for him and attachment to him as to receive him with the determination to receive all he has revealed. The first converts of the Apostles were not converts to a long train of doctrines, but to the gracious and adorable person of Christ. After they had received him it was the business of their lives to learn all they could of him and his doctrine, and do his will.

S. This relieves my mind of what, for a time, was a difficulty. I could not see how Philip received the eunuch with so little ceremony. But I see now that he received everything to Christ, when he said, "I believe that Jesus Christ is the Son of God."

P. It explains every case of conversion in the New Testament. The conversions all took place at the time of the first interview the Apostles had with the penitents. They never sent one away seeking. As a matter of course they did not indoctrinate them in any lengthy system, but presented them the system, as a whole, in the person of Christ. This is presenting the whole gospel in one proposition, so that a man may receive or reject it by saying yes or no, and acting in conformity with that affirmation or denial. Your friend, Mr. H., has blamed us for receiving persons as Philip did the eunuch, upon his confession of his faith in Christ and baptism; but this covers the whole revelation of God to man—includes all that God has revealed to the world. He who makes confession, repents of his sins and is baptized in his name, receives him and all that he and his holy Apostles have taught, and binds himself, by the highest obligations, to do his commandments.

S. Do we not receive remission of sins through the name of Christ?

P. Most certainly, but you must come into his name.

S. Are we not justified by the Spirit of God?

P. Undoubtedly, when we come to his dwelling place.

S. Are we not saved by his life?

P. Beyond all doubt, when we come to his life.

S. And yet his blood cleanses us from sin! How is this?

P. If you will examine every case of baptism you will find that it is always to be administered in the name of the Lord. In baptism, then, the penitent believer takes upon him the name of the Lord. The blood of Christ flowed in his death. When we come into his death we come into his blood. Paul says, "As many as have been baptized into Christ have been baptized into his death." Baptism, then, brings us into the name and into the death of Christ, and consequently to his blood. Paul says to the Corinthians, 'Ye are the temple of God, and the Spirit of God dwells in you." This shows that the spirit dwells in the body, church or temple of God. The life, also, has the same dwelling place. To come, then, to the Spirit and the life, we must come into the body, or into Christ. The Apostle says, we are "baptized into Christ." The man, then, who believes with all his heart in Jesus Christ as the Son of God and the Saviour of the world confesses that faith with the mouth, and is solemnly baptized in the name of the Lord, comes into the name, to the blood, to the Spirit, and into the life of his Lord and Redeemer, who alone can save him.

Not only so, but it is here, and here alone, over the person who believes with all his heart in the Lord Jesus Christ, has repented of his sins, made confession of his faith in Christ, and is about to be buried with his Lord in baptism; that solemn and august formula is authorized to be pronounced: "I baptize you into the name of the Father, and of the Son, and of the Holy Spirit." Here, all Christianity concentrates itself in the great confession made by the penitent; and here, in his first act of obedience, he comes to the blood of the covenant, the Spirit of Christ and his life, and the name of the Father, and of the Son, and of the Holy Spirit, is called upon him, as if to concentrate the whole Divinity upon his poor soul, for its deliverance from sin.

S. Mrs. P., what evidence will I have that I am pardoned?

P. The Lord's own unequivocal promise: "He that believeth and is baptized shall be saved." You have also the evidence of the Apostle, or the Holy Spirit speaking in him: "Repent and be baptized, every one of you, in the name of Jesus Christ, for the remission of sins, and you shall receive the gift of the Holy Spirit." His promise can never fail. Are you not willing to rely upon the promise of God for your salvation?

S. I certainly am, and truly thankful, too, that I have found how I could come to the promise of God with assurance that I should be received. Where shall I go to make confession of my faith in Christ, and be baptized?

P. Attend our church on next Lord's day, and our preacher will baptize you without hesitation.

On the next Lord's day, at an early hour, Sincerity was in the Christian assembly, for the first time, to hear a man who preached nothing but Christ, no doctrine but Christianity, and no name but the name of the Lord. He listened, with intense interest, to a clear and satisfactory discourse on the great elementary principles of Christianity. At the close, he went forward, and in the presence of the assembly, confessed the Saviour of the world. In a few minutes after, he and the preacher stood side by side in the water, some three feet deep, and the large audience standing in breathless silence, while the following words were pronounced: "I baptize you into the name of the Father, and of the Son, and of the Holy Spirit." When these words had been uttered, the preacher gently lowered his noble form beneath the yielding waters. As he raised him up, the audience sang:

"How happy are they who their Saviour obey," etc.

Our young friend rejoiced, believing in the God of his salvation, and the Saviour of the world.

At three o'clock, P. M., of the same day, "when the disciples met together to break bread," Sincerity was present. An Elder of the congregation, arose and read, in an impressive and solemn manner, the hymn commencing with the words:

"And is the gospel peace and love,
Such let our conversation be," etc.

The whole congregation arose, and united in singing the hymn read. The audience was then seated, and the account of the Lord's death was read from John's testimony. The request was then made, that if there were any persons present who had confessed the Lord, and submitted to him as the Saviour of the world, who desire to unite with, or take membership in this individual congregation, they would come forward while the disciples unite in singing the song beginning with the words:

"How sweet, how heav'nly is the sight,
When those that love the Lord.
In one another's peace delight,
And so fulfill the Word," etc.

During the singing, our young friend presented himself in front of the stand, and when the song was ended, the Elder stood before him, and addressed him as follows:

"My dear young brother, I am truly happy to have the privilege of receiving you into this congregation, and trust that the union we this day form, will prove both a blessing to yourself and to the church. You have entered into a solemn covenant with the Lord, and are now bound by the highest and most important obligations that can rest upon a human being, to follow Jesus, to learn of him, to regard him as your infallible Teacher and Master, remembering that he has said, "I will never leave you nor forsake you, but will grant you grace and glory; no good thing will I withhold from you.." He gave himself for you; He laid down his life for you; He made his soul an offering for sin, and in this has evinced his love to you. In this great manifestation of his love to you, he has laid you under eternal obligations to love and serve Him. Your conversion consists not in receiving a long train of speculative doctrines and notions, but in receiving Him who came from heaven—in an identification with him—in placing yourself, as we all are, under Him, as our great Leader and the Captain of our salvation. Look to Him, then; put your whole trust in Him. Read his blessed Word, call upon him every day, and do his commandments, that you may enter by the gates into the city, and have access to the tree of life."

After this address, the church united in singing the song commencing with the words:

> "Blest be the tie that binds
> Our hearts in Christian love,—
> The fellowship of kindred minds,
> Is like to that above," etc.

The members of the church all came forward, and gave him the hand, evincing his cordial and Christian reception, while tears of rejoicing flowed down his manly cheeks. May he serve God all the days of his life.

APPENDIX.

If the reader doubts that *Sincerity* was converted according to the Scriptures, let him read the following list, containing the Lord's own account of all the principal cases of conversions under the apostles and evangelists, recorded in the sacred writings, from the ascension of Christ forward:

"When they heard this, (Peter's discourse), they were pricked in their hearts, and said unto Peter and to the rest of the Apostles, Men and brethren, what shall we do? Then Peter said unto them, Repent and be baptized, every one of you, in the name of Jesus Christ, for the remission of sins, and ye shall receive the gift of the Holy Ghost. For the promise is unto you, and to your children, and to all that are afar off, even as many as the Lord our God shall call. And with many other words did he testify and exhort, saying, Save yourselves from this untoward generation. Then they that gladly received his word were baptized; and the same day there were added unto them about three thousand souls."—Acts ii, 37-41.

In Solomon's portico, at the close of this discourse, Peter said, "Repent ye, therefore, and be converted, that your sins may be blotted out, when the times of refreshing shall come from the presence of the Lord."—Acts iii: 19.

"Then Philip went down to the city of Samaria, and preached Christ unto them. And the people, with one accord, gave heed unto those things, which Philip spake, hearing and seeing the miracles which he did. For unclean spirits, crying with loud voice, came out of many that were possessed with them; and many taken with palsies, and that were lame, were healed. And there was great joy in that city. But there was a certain man, called Simon, who, beforetime in the same city, used sorcery, and bewitched the people of Samaria, giving out that himself was one great one; to whom they all gave heed, from the least to the greatest, saying, This man is the great power of God. And to him they had regard, because that of long time he had bewitched them with sorceries. But when they believed Philip, preaching the things concerning the kingdom of God, and the name of Jesus Christ, they were baptized, both men and women. Then Simon himself, believed also; and when he was baptized, he continued with Philip, and wondered, beholding the miracles and signs which were done."—Acts viii: 5-13.

"And the angel of the Lord spake unto Philip, saying, Arise, and go toward the South, unto the way that goeth down from Jerusalem unto Gaza, which is desert. And he arose and went; and behold, a man of Ethiopia, a eunuch of great authority under Candace, queen of the Ethiopians, who had the charge of all her treasure, and had come to Jerusalem to worship, was returning, and sitting in his chariot read Esaias the Prophet. Then the Spirit said unto Philip, Go near, and join thyself to this chariot. And Philip ran thither to him, and heard him read the Prophet Esaias, and said, Understandest thou what thou readest? And he said, How can I, except some man should guide me? And he desired Philip that he would come up and sit with him. The place of the Scripture which he read was this:,"He was led as a sheep to the slaughter; and like a lamb dumb before the shearer, so opened he not his mouth; in his humiliation, his judgment was taken away; and who shall declare his generation? for his life is taken from the earth.'" And the eunuch answered Philip, and said, I pray thee of whom speaketh the prophet this? of himself, or of some other man? Then Philip opened his mouth and began at the same Scripture, and preached unto him Jesus. And as they went on their way, they came unto a certain water, and the eunuch said, See here is water; what doth hinder me to be baptized? And Philip said, if thou believest with all thy heart, thou mayest. And he answered and said, I believe that Jesus Christ is the Son of God. And he commanded the chariot to stand still, and they went down both into the water, both Philip and the eunuch, and he baptized him. And when they were come out of the water the Spirit of the Lord caught away Philip that the eunuch saw him no more; and he went on his way rejoicing."—Acts viii: 26-39.

"While Peter spake these words, the Holy Ghost fell on all them who heard the word and they of the circumcision, who believed, were astonished, as many as came with Peter, because that on the Gentiles also, was poured out the gift of the Holy Ghost; for they heard them speak with tongues, and magnify God, Then answered Peter, can any man forbid water, that these should not be baptized, who have received the Holy Ghost as well as we? And he commanded them to be baptized in the name of the Lord."—Acts x: 44-48.

"And on the Sabbath, we went out of the city, by a river side, where prayer was wont to be made; and we sat down, and spoke to the woman who resorted thither. And a certain woman named Lydia, a seller of purple, of the city of Thyatira, who worshipped God, heard us; whose heart the Lord opened, that she attended unto the things which were spoken of Paul. And when she was baptized, and her household, she besought us, saying, If ye have judged me to be faithful to the Lord, come into my house and abide there."—Acts xvi: 13-15.

"And at midnight, Paul and Silas prayed, and sang praises unto God; and the prisoners heard them. And suddenly there was a great earthquake, so that the foundations of the prison were shaken; and immediately all the doors were opened and everyone's hands were loosed. And the keeper of the prison awaking out of his sleep, and seeing the prison doors open, he drew out his sword, and would have killed himself, supposing that the prisoners had been fled. But Paul called with a loud voice, saying, Do thyself no harm, for we are all here. Then he called for a light, and sprang In, and came trembling, and fell down before Paul and Silas, and brought them out, and said, Sirs, what must I do to be saved? And they said, Believe on the Lord Jesus Christ, and thou shalt be saved, and thy house. And they spake unto him the word of the Lord, and to all that were in his house. And he took them the same hour of the night, and washed their stripes; and was baptized, he and all his, straightway, And when he had brought them unto his house, he set meat before them, and rejoiced, believing in God with all his house.—Acts xvi: 25-34.

"And it came to pass that while Apollos was at Corinth, Paul having passed through the upper coasts, came to Ephesus; and finding certain disciples, he said unto them, Have ye received the Holy Ghost since ye believed? And they said unto him, We have not so much as heard whether there be any Holy Ghost. And he said unto them, Unto what, then, were ye baptized? And they said, unto John's baptism. Then said Paul, John verily baptized with the baptism of repentance, saying unto the people, that they should believe on him which should come after him, that is, on Jesus Christ. When they heard this, they were baptized in the name of the Lord Jesus."—Acts xix: 1:5.

"And it came to pass, that as I made my journey, and was come nigh unto Damascus, about noon, suddenly there shone from heaven a great light around about me. And I fell unto the ground, and heard a voice saying unto me Saul, Saul, why persecutest thou me? And I answered, Who art thou, Lord? And he said unto me, I am Jesus of Nazareth, whom thou persecuteth. And they that were with me, saw indeed the light, and were afraid; but they heard not the voice of him that spake to me. And I said, What shall I do, Lord? And the Lord said unto me, Arise, and go into Damascus; and there it shall be told thee of all things which are appointed for thee to do. And when I could not see for the glory of that light, being led by the hand of them that were with me, came into Damascus. And one Ananias a devout man, according to the law, having a good report of all the Jews who dwelt there, came unto me, and stood, and said unto me, Brother Saul, receive thy sight. And the same hour I looked up upon him. And he said, The God of our fathers had chosen thee, that thou shouldst know his will, and see that Just One, and shouldst hear the voice of his mouth; for thou shalt be his witness unto all men, of what thou hast seen and heard. And now why tarriest thou? Arise and be baptized, and wash away thy sins, calling on the name of the Lord."—Acts xxii: 6-16.

SCRAP DOCTORS.

IT IS unnecessary for the reader to ask what ancient manuscript I translated the following from. It exposes Scrap Doctors, and that is sufficient for our purpose at present.

It once happened, in a neighborhood where there was a public meeting house, free for all denominations, that four preachers, belonging to different churches, each made an appointment in said house, at the same hour, without knowing of each other's appointment. Consequently, the preachers and members of the four parties, and a goodly number from the world, met at the same time and place, making an extraordinary assembly. The preachers being, or appearing to be in an uncommon good humor, soon amicably agreed, that Brother A. should address the audience, for a short time, first. Brother B. should follow him; then Brother C.; and finally, old Father D. should be permitted to speak; and it was understood that they were to preach on the following text: "Sirs, what must I do to be saved?"

The audience being convened, the speaker having ascended the pulpit, the usual form of singing and prayer was devoutly attended to. Brother A. proceeded to read his text, after which he said:

Dear Brethren and Friends: -I am aware that there is a great variety of sentiment in this audience, and that I cannot declare my conscientious views without crossing some of your opinions, yet, "woe is unto me, if I preach not the Gospel;" and I may add, as an ambassador for Christ, that I cannot violate the conviction of my own conscience. I, however, pledge myself to prove my doctrines by the word of God.

I am now to answer the important question: "What must I do to be saved?" I will come at once to the subject, and take the position that salvation is by repentance and baptism alone. This position is proved by the express word of God, Acts ii: 38. On this occasion the question was asked: "Men and brethren, what shall we do?" Now hear me prove my doctrine. The apostle says, in answer to this question, "Repent and be baptized, every one of you, in the name of Jesus Christ, for the remission of sins." Here, you perceive, they were simply commanded to "Repent and be baptized," and there is not one word about faith, prayer, or anything else. I therefore take it that salvation is by repentance and baptism alone, and I defy the world to refute my position. Do not, therefore, suffer yourselves to be carried about by every wind of doctrine, but accept the doctrine which I have just established by the word of God.

Brother B. next arose and said: "I am happy to appear before you to address you on the great subject of salvation, but I am truly sorry that I cannot accede to the discourse you have just heard, and, although I always avoid controversy, I look upon the doctrine just delivered as extremely dangerous: and professing to be an ambassador of Christ I feel that I should not do justice to my own conscience, were I not to lay before you the truth. Without further preliminaries, I will proceed to state and prove my doctrine.

I take the position that salvation is by *baptism and calling on the name of the Lord alone*, and that there Is neither faith nor repentance in the plan. You remember the conversion of Saul. He inquired: "Lord, what wilt thou have me to do?" The messenger of Jesus said to him, "Arise, and be baptized, and wash away thy sins, calling on the name of the Lord." Here Is the proof of my doctrine. This individual is told what to do to be saved, and not one word about faith or repentance, but he is simply commanded to be baptized, calling on the name of the Lord. No man can get around this proof. Here is the true plan of salvation, proved by the word of God.

Brother C. then arose, and said, I am always anxious to avoid controversy, but I consider the doctrine you have just heard entirely unsupportable, and of most dangerous tendency and should consider myself an unfaithful witness of Jesus, were I not to give my testimony against it. I pronounce the whole of it a delusion. But, as I only have a short time to address you, I will state and prove my doctrine. The brethren who have spoken are both wrong, in connecting repentance, baptism, or prayer with salvation, for we are all saved by faith alone, as I will now proceed to prove from Scripture. The Philippian jailer inquired: "Sirs, what must I do to be saved?" The apostle answered: "Believe on the Lord Jesus Christ, and thou shalt be saved." There is not one word about repentance, baptism or prayer in the text, but he was simply commanded to believe, and was, therefore, saved by faith alone. Here lies the truth, and I defy the world to get around it.

Finally, old Father D. arose and said: "I am truly sorry, my dear brethren, to find you differing so widely, and defending your peculiar notions with such a ranting dogmatism. If you will be so sober as to reflect a few moments, you may easily see where the difficulty lies. You have never yet learned how to take all the Scriptures together. Each one selects his scrap, and detaches it from the other things standing in connection with it, and makes his system of Divinity, out of one detached remark, not remembering that all the items found in the New Testament make up the one great system delivered to man, by the Author of his being. As for Brother A., when speaking of the conversion of the Pentecostians, he forgot to tell you that they already believed, when Peter commanded them to "repent and be baptized;" and Brother B., was very careful not to tell you, when speaking of Paul's conversion, that he already believed, and had been repenting three days, when the messenger of God was sent to him, and commanded him to "arise and be baptized;" and Brother C. was very careful not to mention, when speaking of the conversion of the jailer, that he went the same hour of the night, and was baptized. Peter, on Pentecost, did not command the three thousand to believe, because. they already believed, and Ananias did not command Saul to believe or repent, because he had done it. Paul did command the Jailer to believe, because he had neither believed, repented, been baptized, nor called on the name of the Lord, all of which he had to do to be lawfully saved.

Let Brother A. then, hold on to his repentance and baptism, and Brother B., to his baptism and calling on the name of the Lord, and Brother C., to his faith in the Lord Jesus Christ, and let each one put the whole of these together, and teach the sinner to believe on the Lord Jesus Christ, repent of all his sins. and be baptized, calling on the name of the Lord. Then exhort the disciples to be faithful in keeping all the commandments of the Lord, until death—to "look diligently, lest any man fail of the grace of God.

May God bless you all. Amen."

After the meeting was dismissed, A., B. and C. were invited to a neighboring house to take dinner, where they had the following conversation:

A. Brethren, what do you think of the way that old man rounded off things to-day?

B. I declare I do not know what to think.

C. I think he had a mighty way of smoothing things, and making false doctrine appear like the truth. I am sorry that my brethren were there to hear him, for they appeared to swallow every word with a devouring appetite. What did you think of it, Mr. Landlord?

Landlord. I thought it appeared very reasonable.

A. Brethren, there was something artful in the old fellow's speech, and I saw that about one-half of our best members were almost taken in with his notions. Do you see how plausible he made his doctrine appear? Now, there must be something done to stop him, or he will be constantly getting our members. Now, I recommend that each one of us start round on our respective circuits, and prayerfully and solemnly tell our brethren that D. believes in a water Saviour, and that if a sinner is only dipped under water, all is well; and by thus warning our brethren against his dangerous doctrine, we will keep the people from hearing him.

At this moment, D. stepped in, and said: I am truly sorry to hear you making arrangements to misrepresent the truth. The doctrine which I have the happiness to vindicate, is the only safe doctrine in the world; which I am now prepared to show. If even the Atheist could prove right, which, however, is not possible, then we are entirely safe; for be is bound to admit that we are as happy as he is in this world, and stand equally as good a chance for all beyond. But, if you should prove right, where will the Atheist appear? He is the man who stands exposed to danger.

Again: Suppose the Deist could possibly prove right, and we could find the Bible to be no Revelation from God, even then we are safe, for the Deist is bound to admit the morals of the Bible to be good, and those who obey its dictates are as happy as he in this world and stand a good chance for hereafter. Then if it were possible for him to prove right, he gains nothing, and we lose nothing, here or hereafter. But should he be found mistaken, as he most certainly will, eternal consequences are involved Here we are safe.

Again: Suppose it were possible for the Universalist to prove right, then we are entirely safe, for if all are to be saved it most certainly will include us. "But," says a Universalist, "If I live a Christian life I will be saved anyhow. God will not send me to hell, if there be any, simply because I believed and plead for Universalism." A strange "Christian life," truly, that any man can who, at the same time, believes and pleads for a lie, which will be the condition of all Universalists, if the wicked should go into everlasting punishment in the world to come. The Universalist is on the dangerous side of the question. He hazards everything, without the possibility of gaining anything.

Once more: If faith alone will save us we are safe, for we have as strong faith as any people living. But if "faith without works is dead, being alone," as James teaches, what will become of faith alone, folks?

Still further: If faith and repentance will save us we are safe, for God will not condemn us for obeying any other commands, in addition to these. But if faith and repentance alone will not do, what will become of those who have trifled with other commands of God?

Last of all: The only safe ground is to believe all God has said, and do all he commands, while we live in this world. If we do this the ever-blessed God will be with us while we live, and fort us when we shall find ourselves being cut loose from all our earthly friends, and every worldly consideration, and sinking into eternity. There is a day coming when we will not quibble, and when God will judge between us—to that day I appeal, in view of the course you intend to pursue. "He who knows his Master's will, and does it not, shall be beaten with many stripes."

ADDRESS TO THE READER.

DEAR READERS—There is no subject upon which it is so highly important that we make no mistake as upon the subject of our personal deliverance from sin, guidance, under the divine will, through life, and salvation in heaven. The object of the writer of this little book has been to illustrate the difference between being guided by the confused notions of these times, as seen in the practice of many of the teachers of religion, and the plain and infallible teaching of the Divine Scriptures. The guidance of the living God, as recorded in the Bible, is the only sure directory to purity, holiness and happiness in this life, and eternal blessedness in the life to come. Your only choice for a guide to eternal happiness lies between the Lord, the prophets and apostles, on the one hand, and no guide at all on the other— between the Bible and nothing. For if the Lord, the prophets and apostles fail, if the Bible fails, then all teachers and all books must fail. The Lord, the prophets and apostles are true teachers, or we have none. The Bible is emphatically the guide to heaven, or we have none. The Christian religion is the true religion, or we have none. No other has any claim upon mankind, any credibility, or any intrinsic merit.

There is, therefore, no reason, no possible ground, for any person to hesitate one moment in accepting the only Lord, the only true prophets and apostles, the only infallible book, the only true religion. In Christ, in Christianity, as set forth in the predictions of the prophets and the preaching of the apostles, is the only hope of the world. If this fails all is lost. But, thanks to the giver of every good and perfect gift, it never has and never can fail. The Bible has been the guide and the hope of the best men and women that have ever lived. It has afforded them the highest comforts in life, as well as the strongest, most permanent and gracious assurances of acceptance with God in death. It has never deceived one; It has never disappointed one, nor led one astray. No one has ever lamented adhering to it, imbibing its spirit and obeying its holy precepts; but millions have lamented, mourned, and wailed in most bitter anguish, in deep afflictions and in the hour of death, their indifference, negligence and carelessness in reference to the requirements of the Holy Scriptures. Who has a pen to describe the horrible lamentation, cries and confessions from the lips of the sinful in the hour of death, that rise up to Heaven in consequence of their inattention to the Bible? We have no pen for such a description. We are wholly unable to describe one such scene, and would to God we might never witness another. Nor can we any more describe our own feelings on witnessing such a scene. To hear such an one inquire: "Why have I so wasted my precious time? Why have I been so stupefied? When the lowly Redeemer said, 'Come unto me all ye that labor and are heavy laden, and you shall find rest;' when the Spirit says, 'Whosoever will, let him come, and take of the water of life freely,' what was it that blinded and deluded me so that I did not accept the invitation? When the Lord says, 'All the day long have I stretched forth my hand to a disobedient and gainsaying people,' why did I not flee to him as for life? Why did I not, when in health, seek God?" We say, to hear one in death thus inquiring, is enough, one would suppose, to cause a whole community to repent in sack-cloth and ashes. But will it lead persons to repent? Not often. They will hear all this, and much more, and weep over it, but pursue the same indifferent course as before.

We have witnessed scenes, and heard the declarations of dying sinners that they were lost, ruined and undone, dying without God and without hope. Nay, more—we have seen the hardened and abandoned, and heard their horrid curses in death, and declaring that they already were suffering a foretaste of the future burnings. Such horrid and awful deaths are occurring in numerous instances, and have been witnessed by almost every person of any considerable age and experience. What deep and inexpressible grief such a death causes in a community! But where did anyone devoted to the Lord, the prophets, the apostles and the Bible die such a death? Nowhere. Never was there such a thing since the beginning of time. No! When the righteous die we can say, "Let my latter end be like his."

Do you desire, dear reader, to live in peace with God and man, to die happy, and leave no clouds over the minds of your friends in regard to your future prospects? If you do let me place one single question before you. It is a question asked by our Saviour. It is this: "What think you of Christ? Whose Son is he?" In meditating upon this question you should be guided by the Almighty's own account of his Son, as found in the historic records of Matthew, Mark, Luke and John. These are the divine testimonies of God's own witness concerning Christ. Consult these testimonies carefully and prayerfully, from beginning to end, with the simple question before you, "What think you of Christ? whose Son is he?" Do not try to prove or disprove any doctrine. Do not give yourself any trouble about any doctrine, or any man's view of doctrine, but simply keep your mind upon the person of Christ, and prepare yourself to say from the start what you think of Christ, whose Son he is, and how you desire to act in reference to him. If, when you have examined those testimonies, you resolve to deny him, hate him and oppose him, it is useless to go any further. But if, on the other hand, from all you can learn of him from those testimonies, you love him, have confidence in him, solemnly believe from your heart that he is the Son of God, and the Saviour of the world, and are willing to receive him, you are ready to open another part of the New Testament, that you may learn how to receive him.

This brings us to the second apartment of the New Testament, commonly called the Acts of the Apostles. In this book you will find the first preaching of the Apostles after the ascension of Christ, and the descent of the Holy Spirit to guide the Apostles in all truth; the first conversions to Christianity, the organization of the first churches, and their efforts to carry into practice the New institution. From this book you can learn how the first converts-to Christianity received Christ. If you wish to know that you have received him, according to the will of God, you must receive him as they did, You need nothing more, and must not stop with anything less. When you have received him as they did, and united with the people of God, you wish to know your duty as a disciple or learner of Christ. For this purpose the Lord has arranged another apartment of the New Testament.

This introduces the new convert to the third apartment of his heavenly and infallible guides, the epistles—the letters of the Apostles addressed to those already converted, beginning with the letter to Rome, and embracing all the letters to the Book of Revelation. These holy and infallible letters, dictated by the Spirit of all truth, are to engage the attention, direct the energies, and comfort the child of God through life. He has now only to direct his attention to these holy teachings, and follow them while he lives, and they will guide him to heaven. Here he finds his duty in all the various relations in life clearly and explicitly laid down. Here he finds all the hopes and fears, all the rewards and punishments, placed before him. Here he finds his infallible guide from this world to the land of eternal rest. But when he has followed the Lord and Redeemer many long years, according to the directions laid down in these holy lessons, begins to lean upon the staff and bow toward the grave, his spirit pants for more vivid representation of the future prospects of the saints than he has found in any of the portions of the New Testament yet referred to in this little book. He opens the book of Revelations, and follows John in his splendid vision in the island of Patmos. Here he has a view of the holy city, Jerusalem, the tree of life, the river of the water of life, the immortal and glorified inhabitants; where there is no sickness, sorrow, pain and death, but where praises to God and the Lamb ascend forever and ever. Here he beholds golden streets, and jasper walls clear as crystal. In his body, bending with infirmity, and but dim mortal eyes, by the aid of Revelation he sees the land of immortality and the inhabitants of the world of bliss.

What a book, then, the New Testament is; a book adapted to the unbeliever, containing an apartment filled with the sacred testimonies leading him to believe in his Saviour; a second apartment following, showing him how to receive the Lord, in his conversion to Christianity a third apartment, guiding him through from his conversion to his death, in humble submission to the divine will, and, at the close, a full representation of the eternal glories of the redeemed, directing his attention to the day when he shall join with the pure and holy of the companions of his youthful days; the good and virtuous of all ages; the prophets and the Apostles, with Jesus his Redeemer, and God the Almighty Father.

Many thousands who shall read this little book we shall never see in this world, but, through the grace of God, we trust we shall in the holy city, the New Jerusalem, that John saw descend from God out of heaven. The hope of seeing those we love, and Jesus, who loved us and gave himself for us; of being like him, and dwelling with him in the presence of his Father, is the anchor to the soul that enters to that within the veil, and bears up the drooping spirits of the children of God.

To him who loved us, and washed us from our sins in his own blood, be honor and power everlasting. Amen.[164]

---

[164] Benjamin Franklin, <u>SINCERITY SEEKING THE WAY TO HEAVEN</u>, (F. L. ROWE Publisher: Cincinnati, Ohio), 1856.

APPENDIX B

Elisha Brooks and Elias Sias
Begin in Gratiot County[165]

by
Robert Laurence Girdwood

---

[165] This section was reprinted from Bob Girdwood's <u>The Stone-Campbell Movement In Michigan</u>. Permission to reprint was granted.

Elisha Brooks and Elias Sias Begin in Gratiot County

In 1855 Elisha Brooks moved from Indiana, from just north of Ft. Wayne, to claim 160 acres in Pine Township, immediately north of St. Louis, Michigan. He found a family named Sias recently settled in the area and a good friendship began.

The Brooks family had been members of a Church of Christ at Newville, Indiana, and missed the fellowship of like-minded Christian people here in central Michigan. They found the Sias family to be good people although not yet committed Christians. A warm friendship began to blossom.

(Following is partly an historical novel accounting of what probably happened)

"What is this I hear about your son Elias getting romantic?" Elisha queried of father Sias one day as they rested from clearing timber from another acre of land. "He strikes me as being one of the best young men we have in this part of the country. Sure hope he's not planning to marry and move away."

"I think his love of these woods is deep enough already that we can count on his staying around. And mother and I are pleased that he has picked a girl with some beautiful Christian principles." Father Sias smiled as he considered a possible partnership with his son. Everything looked to be heading in the right direction.

The wedding was a big affair. About everyone in the area came out to celebrate. It was one of the first weddings in Gratiot County and their frontier was becoming civilized. They didn't have much choice of preachers to tie the knot since the Methodists were the only ones who had regular meetings and regular visits by a preacher.

It was in fact during the wedding days that the plans had been set for the Methodist camp meeting in 1856 at St Louis. Elias and his bride felt personally interested. After all it had been planned while they were uniting their lives and beginning to develop their new family ideals, life-style and faith.

Elias and his wife talked a lot about what part faith and the church should have in building a marriage and home. When camp meeting time came they had already decided they would commit their lives to the Lord. Their commitment was not to denominational doctrine but to Christ. And the Methodists were the only Christians around.

Elisha Brooks and his family also attended the meeting. They were pleased to see the Siases there and to see Elias beginning his new home with Christ as the heart of its strength.

The next day Elisha dropped by the young Siases to offer his support and encouragement. He brought along a tract that had meant much to him and helped his spiritual growth.

"Just wanted to drop this by for you to look at," offered Elisha, "it has been of help to me and I believe you'll enjoy reading it. No hurry to get it back. Check it out and let me know what you think."

"Thanks much." Elias knew the Brooks were fine Christian people and had a beautiful marriage. "If these ideas have helped to make your home the strong and happy place that it is, we'll be very much wanting to see what it says."

In fact, that very evening, the Siases sat down together to begin study of "Sincerity Seeking the Way to Heaven" by Benjamin Franklin. Elias had his wife hunt up all the Bible references as they read.

"I'm interested in this idea that everyone ought to be simply Christians without being some brand kind." Elias was testing the ideas on his wife. "Am I correct when I guess that you feel the same as I do?"

"Oh yes," responded the new Mrs. Sias, "but it looks to me like there are a couple of things we'll have to work out before we can put it into practice the way the Bible says. First, I'm wondering how we can be just plain Christians without being Methodists. After all that is the most active church around here. And second, these Bible verses about baptism speak differently than what we heard at the camp meeting."

"Let's have the Brooks over for dinner as soon as we can," Elias had other questions even beyond those of his wife. "If you'd like, I'll drop by their place tomorrow and invite them." "That would be good. I'm not sure I know how to get everything together for feeding company, but there is no time like now to learn."

Elias loved his wife more every day. Her heart, mind and life were forever lifting him to new dreams of a happy and full life together for years to come. Of course, she also challenged him to think in broader dimensions and to be sure before he accepted new conclusions and made changes in his life and future. Now he had to see Elisha and arrange their dinner date.

"Be happy to come by for a good meal and hopefully I can help you with some of your questions." Elisha was thrilled at their growing friendship.

A couple of days later they gathered for an excellent meal and by its end the new cook was at ease. Mrs Brooks had been able to assist in the few details where new brides need encouragement and the two of them made quick sport washing the dishes. Their husbands had already begun to probe the Biblical concerns.

"Let's go over those scriptures again about baptism." suggested Elias. "I want the wife to use her good sense to be sure we cover all of our questions." As the four of them gathered around the table where they could lay out their Bibles, the tract, and set the coffee pot, the study became more intense.

"If I understand what the Bible says," began Elias, "wife and I need to be immersed because the sprinkling proposed by the Methodists just isn't enough."

"But our decision to accept the Lord was real and sincere." offered Elias' wife.

"I'm sure no one will question your sincerity in the commitments you made in the camp meeting." Elisha assured them. "You believed and put into practice everything you heard and knew. The point here is that there is more needed if you want to accept and practice everything the Bible says. And that includes immersion. If I understand correctly, that doesn't make you any kind of denominational Christian. It just does what the Lord asks."

"I'll ask the United Brethren preacher to immerse us when he comes by here next week." Elias was not one to let things drift, especially when it seemed to be as important as this was.

Elias was very disappointed the next Sunday when the preacher dismissed his concern and questions as miscellaneous detail. Elias then asked him, since he and his wife had decided immersion was important, if he would baptize them by immersion. The United Brethren preacher said, "No."

Immediately, the Siases went to ask the Brooks what to do. Elisha had little formal education and only the tract besides his Bible and some of the questions Elias had were beyond Elisha's knowledge. Finally the idea came.

"Elias, if you could give me a couple of days work. As soon as we can get some of the farming done up ahead, why don't you take my saddle horse and ride to Newville, Indiana, where Randall Faurot preaches and leads a Christian school? He can answer your questions and I know you will be impressed by his faith. Give me a week. Then you can bring him back up here to talk to us all."

The camp meeting was now several weeks back. The tract Brooks had given Sias had by now been read over and checked out by several others of those who had made commitments at the meeting. At least three of four other couples also felt as did the Siases. Elias became their leader and he prepared for the journey south to seek out answers to their questions. Christianity was important to them all and they were not about to let things slide and be forgotten.

At the crack of dawn one morning as the Siases were finishing their breakfast, they saw Elisha Brooks bringing his saddle horse. Within the hour, Elias was riding toward Newville, Indiana. About noon, horse and rider had reached Maple Rapids, about 20 miles away. While Elias visited over coffee at the Inn there, he told his story.

"What you're talking about is exactly the same story I have heard from several people out of the Muir/Lyons area about 15 miles down the Maple River." offered one of the men. "They've begun a new town and lumbering operation just this side of the river from Lyons. I believe every one of the company are from the Churches of Christ in northeast Ohio. They call themselves Restorationists and their feelings about baptism by immersion are the same as yours. In fact, they brought a preacher by the name of Isaac Errett along for the sole purpose of setting up a church there and evangelizing this whole area."

Elias liked the idea. "Any specific directions?"

"You'll find them easy. They've been scouting the whole country west of here and have bought up thousands of acres north of Muir and up along Fish Creek. The creek heads north only about five miles down the river. Just follow the Maple River to its junction with the Grand River and everyone will know where to find your man Errett. A guy by name of Ambros Soule is the head of the lumber company."

It all sounded good and credible to Elias, so he headed west down the Maple River. Shortly he saw some of the land scouts' marks at Fish Creek but had to ride all the way into Muir before he found people who knew. Heartbreak may not be too strong a word to express Elias' feelings when he learned that Errett was out of the area and would not be back for several days.

"But I like to preach" confessed "Uncle Ben" Soule, one of the partners, "and while I may not be as educated as Brother Errett, I'll bet we can figure out some of your answers. Come on over to the house. Mrs Soule will fix us a good dinner and you can stay the night."

Elias liked Ben Soule immediately and was indeed impressed with his knowledge of the Bible. Here was a businessman who knew the Lord as well as successful business. Quick and easily "Uncle Ben" took the young student Elias under his wing and guided him into the depths of Biblical wisdom that would put many a preacher to shame.

After they had talked for two or three hours Ben asked, "Are you aware that you don't have to be a clergyman or an 'official' preacher to baptize people?"

Elias had never even thought about this. He had just supposed that this was preacher work. They studied the idea for another hour or two. Finally, Elias was convinced and suggested, "Why don't you come back with me to St Louis and baptize all twelve of us? We're ready! And I'd like you to meet Elisha Brooks. He's the one that got me started on this quest, you know."

"I'd be delighted to. Errett will be crushed that he missed the chance. Maybe this will help convince him to stay home and reap the harvest the good Lord has ready right here. And I need to check out some details up on Fish Creek anyway."

And so it was "Uncle Ben" Soule who baptized those first 12 people (Elias and eleven others) up at St. Louis. He really didn't like to preach but he was one of the best teachers alive and he taught/preached. And how he did enjoy baptizing people into Christ. He did the baptizing the next night and spent a whole day teaching his heart out to the new converts. Before he left St. Louis he suggested in his powerful way that Brooks and Sias ought to do some preaching up in Gratiot County. He was sure Brooks could lead out much as he was down in Lyons/Muir and he just knew that young Sias was a gifted preacher if he ever saw one. And he hadn't even heard him preach yet. "Uncle Ben" couldn't wait for Errett to get back. Did he have a God-sighting story to tell him!

Brooks and Sias kept the fellowship around St. Louis alive and spiritually growing. A new friend of theirs about four miles east by name of A V Packer began a Sunday School in his home at Forest Hill. For the next two years the two groups studied and grew in maturity. There was little growth in numbers. This was one of those times when "remaining faithful" was the business at hand in Gratiot. And this would be true for more than two years.

ORIGIN & DEVELOPMENT OF THE SINNER'S PRAYER[166]

Salvation in the Beginning

In the beginning, no one in the Bible ever prayed to receive their salvation. They did, however, hear the gospel and believed it; repented of their sins; confessed Jesus as their Lord, and were immersed in water for the forgiveness of their sins.[167]At the conclusion of the first sermon preached, on the first day of the church, the apostle Peter told the crowd,

> "Repent and be baptized everyone of you in the name of Jesus Christ for the forgiveness of your sins. And you will receive the gift of the Holy Spirit. This promise is for you and your children and for all who are far off — for all whom the Lord our God will call." With many other words he warned them; and he pleaded with them, "Save yourselves from this corrupt generation." Those who accepted his message were baptized, and about three thousand were added to their number that day.[168]

This is the model of salvation the early church practiced for many years. Early church fathers like Justin Martyr (130 AD), Irenaeus (175 AD), and Tertullian (180 AD)[169] taught that in baptism by immersion one is regenerated by God for the remission of sins.

---

[166] Steven Francis Staten has written several articles about the origin of the Sinner's Prayer. With his permission I have reprinted one of his documents in this chapter. I have extended Mr. Staten's outline and provided citations to support it. See: "The Sinner's Prayer," www.bible.ca/g-sinners-prayer.htm. Internet. (Retrieved August 10, 2014). Stephen F. Staten © Copyright, 1997, reprinted with permission.

[167] See the chart at the end "Conversions In the Book of Acts" for examples of how individuals received salvation. Wayne Jackson notes, "A careful study of the cases of conversion in the book of Acts will reveal that in not a single instance is the sinner instructed to "pray" for his or her salvation." Wayne Jackson, "The Sinner's Prayer-Is It Biblical?" Christiancourier.com. Internet. (Retrieved November 16, 2014).

[168] Acts 2:38-41. New International version.

[169] Philip Schaff, "Infant Baptism," History of the Christian Church; Ante-Nicene Christianity AD 100-325, Volume II, (William B. Eerdmans, 1910), 258-262.

No one is certain when the practice of infant baptism began, however allusions to it appear by 200 AD. From at least the 3rd century onward, Christians baptized infants as standard practice, although some preferred to postpone baptism until late in life, so as to ensure forgiveness for all their preceding sins. Philip Schaff notes that by the fifth and sixth centuries, infant baptism had replaced adult believers baptism by immersion in the church up to the Reformation of the sixteenth century.[170]

The Reformation

At the beginning of the sixteenth century, attitudes toward the Catholic church were changing. There was a general consensus growing in Christendom to return the church back to the Bible. A small faction called Anabaptists[171] denied the validity of infant baptism and rejected all Roman Catholic baptism as valid.[172] They re-baptized those whom they regarded as not having received any Christian initiation at all, and claimed that their baptism after profession of faith was the recipient's first legitimate baptism.[173] In response, the Roman Catholic church hated and persecuted the Anabaptists.

The Reformers[174] were sympathetic to the Anabaptists but had mixed feelings about infant baptism. Most felt it was wrong but were not willing to give it up. Huldrych Zwingli is the one who would ultimately shape future opinions about baptism. Zwingli preached that baptism was a symbol of the New Covenant as circumcision was to the Old. In time, this would become the accepted view in modern Evangelical Christianity.[175]

Although things weren't ideal after the Reformation, for the first

---

[170] Philip Schaff, "Baptism," (History of the Christian Church; Nicene & Post Nicene Christianity AD 311-600, Volume III.), 483.

[171] Anabaptist means "re-baptizers" in the Greek.

[172] Walter Klaassen, Anabaptism in Outline, (Herald Press, 1981), 168.

[173] "Theology of Anabaptism," Wikipedia, Internet. (Retrieved September 12, 2014).

[174] Martin Luther, John Calvin, Huldrych Zwingli, and Desiderius Erasmus were the most noted Protestant Reformers.

[175] Jack W. Cottrell, "Baptism According to the Reformed Tradition," Baptism and the Remission of Sins, David W. Flecher, editor, (College Press, 1990), 58.

time in over a thousand years the general populace was reading the Scriptures. By the early 1600s, one hundred years after the Reformation was initiated, there were various branches of European Christendom that followed national lines. For instance, Germans followed Martin Luther. There were also Calvinists (Presbyterian), the Church of England (Episcopalian), various branches of Anabaptists and, of course, the Roman church (Catholics). Most of these groups were trying to revive the waning faith of their already traditionalized denominations. However, a consensus had not been reached on issues like rebirth, baptism or salvation--even between Protestants.

The majority still held to the validity of infant baptism even though they disagreed on its significance. The influence of preachers eventually led to the popular notion that one was forgiven at infant baptism but not yet reborn. Most Protestants were confused or ambivalent about the connection between rebirth and forgiveness.[176]

Post Reformation - The Great Awakening

The Great Awakening was the result of fantastic preaching occurring in Europe and the eastern colonies during the early to mid 1700s. Though ambivalent on the practice of baptism, Great Awakening preachers created an environment that made man aware of his need for an adult confession experience. The experiences that people sought were varied. Jonathan Edwards, George Whitfield and John Wesley furthered ideas of radical repentance and revival. Although there is much to be learned from their messages, they did not solve the problems of the practices associated with baptism and conversion.

Eventually, the following biblical passage written to lukewarm Christians became a popular tool for the conversion of non-Christians:

"To the angel of the church in Laodicea write: These are the words of the Amen, the faithful and true witness, the ruler of God's creation. ....Those whom I love I

---

[176] Thomas R. Schreiner and Shawn D. Wright, <u>BELIEVER'S BAPTISM SIGN OF THE NEW COVENANT IN CHRIST</u>, (Nashville: B&H Publishing Co., 2006), 218.

rebuke and discipline. So be earnest, and repent. Here I am! I stand at the door and knock. If anyone hears my voice and opens the door, I will come in and eat with him, and he with me." (Revelation 3:14-20)

This passage was written explicitly for lukewarm Christians. Now consider how a lecturer named John Webb misused this passage in the mid 1700s as a basis of evangelizing non-Christians:

"Here is a promise of Union to Christ; in these words, I will come in to him. i.e. If any Sinner will but hear my Voice and open the Door, and receive me by Faith, I will come into his Soul, and unite him to me, and make him a living member of that my mystical body of which I am the Head."[177]

Preachers heavily relied on Revelation 3:20. By using the first-person tense while looking into the sinner's eyes, preachers began to speak for Jesus as they exhorted, "If you would just let me come in and dine with you, I would accept you." John Webb in 1741 elevated this approach to a mass appeal with heavy emotionalism.

Heathens who had never been baptized responded with the same or even greater sorrow than churchgoers. As a result, more and more preachers of Christendom concluded that baptism was merely an external matter--only an outward sign of an inward grace. This was the idea Huldrych Zwingli put forth several years earlier. Nowhere in church history was such a belief recorded.

Eleazar Wheelock (Mourner's Seat)

It is documented that in 1741 a minister named Eleazar Wheelock had utilized a technique called the Mourner's Seat.[178] As far as one can tell, he would target sinners by having them sit in the front bench

---

[177] John Webb, <u>Christ's Suit to the Sinner</u>, (Boston: S. Kneeland & T. Green, 1871), 14.
[178] Joel L. Watts, "Easy Believism," Unsettledchristianity.com. Internet. (Retrieved November 19, 2014).

(pew). During the course of his sermon, "salvation was looming over their heads." He was criticized by his contemporaries for stimulating excessive emotion and fervor in his preaching.[179] Afterwards, the sinners were typically quite open to counsel and exhortation. In fact, as it turns out, they were susceptible to whatever prescription the preaching doctor gave to them. According to eyewitnesses, false conversions were multiplied. Charles Wesley had some experience with this practice, but it took nearly a hundred years for this tactic to take hold.

Cane Ridge (Beginning of Revival Techniques)

In 1801 there was a sensational revival in Cane Ridge, Kentucky that lasted for weeks. Allegedly, people barked, rolled over in the aisles and became delirious because there were long periods without food in the intense heat. It resulted in the extreme use and abuse of emotions as thousands left Kentucky with wild notions about rebirth. Today it is generally viewed as a mockery to Christianity.

The excesses in Cane Ridge produced expectations for preachers and those seeking religious experience. A Second Great Awakening, inferior to the first, was beginning in America.[180] Preachers were enamored with the idea that they could cause (manipulate) people into conversion. One who witnessed such nineteenth century hysteria was J. V. Coombs (a Disciples of Christ minister, 1849) who complained of the technique:

> "The appeals, songs, prayers and the suggestion from the preacher drive many into the trance state. I can remember in my boyhood days seeing ten or twenty people laying unconscious upon the floor in the old country church. People called that conversion. Science knows it is mesmeric influence, self-hypnotism ... It is

---

[179] Roderick Beebe Sullivan Jr. "Rev. Eleazar Wheelock," Wheelockgenealogy.com. Internet. (Retrieved November 19, 2014).
[180] Leroy Garrett, The Stone-Campbell Movement, (College Press, 1981), 75.

sad that Christianity is compelled to bear the folly of such movements."[181]

The Cane Ridge Meeting became the paradigm for revivalists for decades.[182] A lawyer named Charles Finney came along a generation later to systemize the Cane Ridge experience through the use of Wheelock's Mourner's Seat and Scripture.

Charles Finney (Anxious Seat)[183]

It wasn't until about 1835 that Charles Grandison Finney (1792-1875) emerged to champion the system utilized by Eleazar Wheelock. Shortly after his own conversion, he left his law practice and would become a minister, a lecturer, a professor, and a traveling revivalist. He took the Mourner's Seat practice, which he called the Anxious Seat, and developed a theological system around it. He is recognized as the father of the altar call.[184] Finney was straightforward about his purpose for this technique and wrote the following comment near the end of his life:

> "The church has always felt it necessary to have something of this kind to answer this very purpose. In the days of the apostles, baptism answered this purpose. The gospel was preached to the people, and then all those who were willing to be on the side of Christ, were called out to be baptized. It held the place that the anxious seat does now as a public manifestation of their determination to be Christians"[185]

---

[181] J. V. Coombs, Religious Delusions: A Psychic Study, (Cincinnati: Standard Publishing Company, 1904), 92ff.

[182] Mark Galli, "Revival at Cane Ridge," Christianitytoday.com, Issue 45, 1995. Internet. (Retrieved November 20, 2014).

[183] "Charles Grandison Finney," Wikipedia, Internet. (Retrieved December 6, 2014).

[184] Patrick McIntyre, "History of the Sinner's Prayer," You Tube Video. Internet. (Retrieved November 12, 2014).

[185] Notice the theological shift in Finney's remarks - the anxious seat replaces baptism. Charles G. Finney, Lectures On Revivals Of Religion, (New York: Leavitt, Lord & Co., 1835), 248.

Finney made many enemies because of this innovation. The Anxious Seat practice was considered to be a psychological technique that manipulated people to make a premature profession of faith. It was considered to be an emotional conversion influenced by some of the preachers' animal magnetism. Certainly it was a precursor to the techniques used by many twentieth century televangelists.

In opposition to Finney's movement, John Nevin, a Protestant minister, wrote a book called The Anxious Bench. He intended to protect the denominations from this novel deviation. He called Finney's New Measures "heresy", a "Babel of extravagance", "fanaticism", and "quackery". He also said, "With a whirlwind in full view, we may be exhorted reasonably to consider and stand back from its destructive path."[186] It turns out that Nevin was somewhat prophetic. The system that Finney admitted had replaced biblical baptism, is the vertebrae for the popular plan of salvation that was made normative in the twentieth century.

Dwight Moody (Inquiry Rooms)

However, it wasn't until the end of Finney's life that it became evident to everyone and himself that the Anxious Bench approach led to a high fallout rate. By the 1860s Dwight Moody (1837-1899) was the new apostle in American evangelicalism. He took Finney's system and modified it. Instead of calling for a public decision, which tended to be a response under pressure, he asked people to join him and his trained counselors in a room called the Inquiry Room.[187] Though Moody's approach avoided some of the errors encountered in Finneyism, it was still a derivative, or stepchild, of the Anxious Bench system.

In the Inquiry Room, the counselors asked the possible convert some questions, taught him from scripture, and then prayed with him. The idea that prayer was at the end of the process had been loosely associated with conversion in the 1700s. A possible early version of a Sinner's Prayer is found in Pilgrim's Progress by John Bunyun, published

[186] John Williamson Nevin, The Anxious Bench, (Chartersburg: German Reformed Church, 1844), 7.
[187] Lyle Dorsett, Profile in Faith: D. L. Moody, (Billy Graham Chair of Evangelism), Internet article.

in 1678.[188] By the late 1800s it was standard technique for 'receiving Christ' as Moody's influence spread across both the United States and the United Kingdom. This was where a systematic Sinner's Prayer began, but was not called as such until the time of Billy Sunday.

The Twentieth Century
R. A. Torrey (Sinner's Prayer)

R. A. Torrey succeeded Moody's Chicago-based ministry after his death in 1899. He modified Moody's approach to include "on the spot" street conversions. Torrey popularized the idea of instant salvation with no strings attached, even though he never intended as much. Nonetheless, "Receive Christ, now, right here" became part of the norm.[189] From that time on it became more common to think of salvation outside of church or a life of Lordship. Torrey is considered the father of the Sinner's Prayer.[190]

Billy Sunday and the Pacific Garden Mission

Meanwhile in Chicago, Billy Sunday, a well-known baseball player from Iowa, had been converted in the Pacific Garden Mission. The Mission was Chicago's most successful implementation of Moody's scheme. Eventually, Sunday left baseball to preach. He had great public charm and was one of the first to mix ideas of entertainment with ministry. By the early 1900s he had become a great well-known crusade leader. In his crusades he popularized the Finney-Moody method and included a bit of a circus touch.

After fire and brimstone sermons, heavy moralistic messages with political overtones, and humorous if not outlandish behavior, salvation was offered. Often it was associated with a prayer, and at other times a person was told they were saved because they simply walked down his tabernacle's "sawdust trail" to the front where he was standing. In time

---

[188] "Sinner's Prayer," <u>Wikipedia</u>, Ibid. (Retrieved September 10, 2014).
[189] R. A. Torrey, <u>How To Bring Men To Christ</u>, (Fleming H. Revell Co., 1893), p. 35.
[190] Bill J. Leonard, <u>A Sense of the Heart</u>, (Abingdon Press, 2013), p.63.

people were told they were saved because they publicly shook Sunday's hand, acknowledging that they would follow Christ.[191]

Billy Sunday died in 1935, leaving behind hundreds of his imitators. More than anything else, Billy Sunday helped crusades become acceptable to all denominations, which eventually led to a change in their theology. Large religious bodies sold out on their reservations toward these new conversion practices to reap the benefits of potential converts from the crusades because of the allure of success.

Billy Sunday often bragged about his ignorance of church history and theology. One of his famous statements was "I don't know any more about theology than a jack-rabbit does about ping-pong, but I'm on the way to glory."[192] This is highly significant because the Anxious Seat phenomenon and offshoot practices were not rooted in scripture nor in the early church.

Billy Graham

Billy Graham and his crusades were the next step in the evolution of things. Billy Graham was converted in 1936 at a Sunday-styled crusade. By the late 1940s it was evident to many that Graham would be the champion of evangelicalism. His crusades summed up everything that had been done from the times of Charles Finney through Billy Sunday, except that he added respectability that some of the others lacked. In the 1950s, Graham's crusade counselors were using a prayer that had been sporadically used for some time. It began with a prayer from his Four Steps to Peace With God.[193] The original four-step formula came during Billy Sunday's era in a tract called Four Things God Wants You to Know.[194] The altar call system of Graham had been refined by a

---

[191] Diana Severance, Billy Sunday Found the Prairie, Christian History Institute.com. Internet. (Retrieved September 6, 2014).

[192] Tom Nettles, "Billy Sunday, Part 3: Jack Rabbits and Creeds," FOUNDERS, (March 24, 2015). Internet. (Retrieved May 23, 2016).

[193] An example of this practice is noted as late as 2005 in the New York Crusade. Billy Graham, Living in God's Love - The New York Crusade, (New York: G. P. Putnam's Sons, 2005), 93-95.

[194] "Billy Sunday," Wikipedia, https://en.wikipedia.org/wiki/Billy_Sunday. Internet. (Retrieved April 3, 2016).

precise protocol of music, trained counselors, and a speaking technique all geared to help people "accept Christ as Savior."[195]

Later, in 1977 Billy Graham published a now famous work entitled, How to Be Born Again. For all the Scripture he used, he never once uses the hallmark rebirth event in the second chapter of the book of Acts.[196] The cataract (blind spot) kept him away from the most powerful conversion event in all Scripture. It is my guess that its emphasis on baptism and repentance for the forgiveness of sins was incompatible with his approach.

Bill Bright (Campus Crusade)

In the late 1950s Bill Bright came up with the exact form of the currently popular Four Spiritual Laws so that the average believer could take the crusade experience into the living room of their neighbor. Of course, this method ended with the Sinner's Prayer.[197] Those who responded to crusades and sermons could have the crusade experience at home when they prayed,

"Lord Jesus, I need You. Thank You for dying on the cross for my sins. I open the door of my life and receive You as my Savior and Lord. Thank You for forgiving my sins and giving me eternal life. Take control of the throne of my life. Make me the kind of person You want me to be."

The Living Bible and Beyond

By the late 1960s it seemed that nearly every evangelical was printing some form of the Four Spiritual Laws in the last chapter of their books. Even a Bible was printed with this theology inserted into God's Word.

---

[195] "Billy Graham," Wikipedia, https://en.wikipedia.org/Billy_Graham. Internet. (Retrieved October 10, 2014).

[196] Gene Edwards, a former Billy Graham counselor, stated that the Crusade used R. A. Torrey evangelistic methods. Jan Blodgett, Protestant Evangelical Literary Culture and Contemporary Society, (Connecticut: Greenwood Press, 1954), 152.

[197] An example of this is seen in Josh McDowell, Evidence That Demands A Verdict, (Campus Crusade for Christ, 1972), 385.

Thus, in the 1960s, the Living Bible's translation became the translation of choice for the crusades as follows:

> "Even in his own land and among his own people, the Jews, he was not accepted. **Only a few welcome and received him**. But to all who received him, he gave the right to become children of God. **All they needed to do was to trust him to save them. All those who believe this are reborn!** --not a physical rebirth resulting from human passion or plan--but from the will of God."(John 1:11-13, Living Bible)[198]

The bolded words have no support at all in the original Greek. They are a blatant insertion placed by presuppositions of the translator, Kenneth Taylor. In defense of Taylor's original motives, the Living Bible was created primarily with children in mind. However, the publishers should have corrected the misleading verse in the 1960s. They somewhat cleared it up in the newer LB in the 1990s, only after the damage has been done. For decades mainstream evangelicals were using the LB and circular reasoning to justify such a strong 'trusting moment' as salvation, never knowing their Bible was corrupted.

A whole international enterprise of publishers, universities and evangelistic associations were captivated by this method. The phrases, "Receive Christ," and "Trust Jesus as your personal savior," filled airwaves, sermons, and books. James Kennedy's Evangelism Explosion counselor-training program helped make this concept of conversion an international success.[199] Missionaries everywhere were trained with Sinner's Prayer theology. Evangelicalism had the numbers, the money, the television personas of Graham and Kennedy, and any attempt to purport a different plan of salvation would be decried as cultic and "heresy."

Most evangelicals are ignorant of where their practice came from or how Christians from other periods viewed biblical conversion. C. S.

---

[198] Life Application Bible - The Living Bible, (Tyndale Publishers, 1971), 233.
[199] D. James Kennedy, Evangelism Explosion, (Wheaton: Tyndale House Publishers, 1970), 54.

Lewis regarded it as chronological snobbery when we don't review our beliefs against the conclusions of others.[200] While most do this unknowingly, evangelicals are skewing church auditoriums all over the world from a clear picture of conversion with a nonsensical practice.

IS IT BIBLICAL?

In light of its shady historical roots, it may seem silly to ask, is the Sinner's Prayer biblical? No! There is not one example of Jesus, the apostles or anyone else ever asking an unsaved person to pray and ask Jesus into their heart. There is not a single verse or passage of Scripture, whether in a narrative account or in prescriptive or descriptive texts, regarding the use of a "Sinner's Prayer" in evangelism.[201] However, proponents of the use of the Sinner's Prayer will cite several passages of scripture in a failed attempt to support the unbiblical practice.

There are five primary texts cited by proponents: Matthew 7:7; Luke 18:10-14; Romans 10:9-10; 1 John 1:9; and Revelation 3:20.[202] When we apply basic interpretation rules, two observations are easily made. First, none of these texts are used in an evangelism context in "their" setting. Second, in none of these texts are the hearers encouraged to pray to receive salvation.

On the surface it would appear that the Luke 18 passage is a prime example of salvation by prayer. However, context does not allow this interpretation. First, the two men who went to the temple to pray were Jewish men who believed in God and worshiped Him. Second, their occupations had nothing to do with their salvation. Tax collectors were Jews who were employed by the Romans. Even though the Jews considered tax collectors in the same category as sinners, God did not. Third, the issue in the text was attitude, not salvation. The Pharisee gloried in his piety whereas the tax collector humbled himself before God and was justified. Jesus used that parable to teach his disciples the

---

[200] C. S. Lewis, "Surprised By Joy," p. 206, <u>Wikipedia</u>, Internet (Retrieved November 20, 2014).

[201] Tony Miano and Matt Slick, "Is the Sinner's Prayer biblical or not?" <u>Christian Apologetics and Research Ministry</u>, https://carm.org/sinners-prayer. Internet. (Retrieved 18 March 2013).

[202] Ibid.

proper attitude of those who worship God. Proper exegesis does not allow this text to be a biblical example of a Sinner's Prayer.

Current Evangelical Consternation

One of the issues debated at the 2012 Southern Baptist Conference was the use of the Sinner's Prayer in Baptist churches. Mega church minister, David Platt[203] was the most outspoken against its use. Calling it "superstitious," Platt said the emphasis upon the Sinner's Prayer is "unbiblical and damning."[204] In reaction to "easy believism," internationally known Southern Baptist Evangelists Paul Washer, John MacArthur and others have been publicly opposed for their adamant position that salvation prayers do not guarantee salvation.[205] Meanwhile, Steve Gaines, minister of Bellevue Baptist Church in Memphis, Tennessee, called the Sinner's Prayer representative of God's New Covenant.

Although the Convention voted in favor of its use, twenty percent of the votes were against it. Eric Hankins, minister of First Baptist Church in Oxford, Mississippi, in response to the vote remarked, "I'm not going to say the Sinner's Prayer is the only way for people to come to faith. But for me, after 20 years of ministry, it's a pretty typical way."

It is astounding that those who profess to believe in the Bible and purport to teach it accurately would take such a cavalier approach to one of the most important elements of the Christian faith.

OUR POSITION

It has always been our desire in the Independent Christian Churches and Churches of Christ to follow the plan of salvation as defined in the New Testament. Restoration Movement Reformers of the nineteenth

---

[203] David Platt is the Senior Minister at Brook Hills Baptist church in Birmingham, Alabama.

[204] Ted Olsen, "Southern Baptists Debate the Sinner's Prayer," Christianity Today, June 20, 2012, ChristianityToday.com. Internet. (Retrieved September 10, 2014).

[205] Sean Harris, "The Sinner's Prayer: Biblical Or Extra-Biblical," Http://pastorseansblog.blogspot.com/2010/07/sinner's-prayer.html. Internet. (Retrieved November 17, 2014).

century rejected the emotional sensationalism of the revivalist preachers. Their message was a clear and simple one. Most noted of the Reformers was Walter Scott. "Scott called on people to accept Jesus Christ as the Messiah and Son of God. Then he said that the steps to salvation were like pointing to the fingers on your hand - faith, repentance, baptism, remission of sins, and the gift of the Holy Spirit."[206] Scott called his plan of salvation the Ancient Gospel.[207]

Over the years our churches embraced Scott's presentation of the plan of salvation with a few modifications. In what follows is our understanding of what the New Testament teaches about how an individual receives salvation.

- Salvation is offered to mankind through God's grace (Eph. 2:4-5).
- In order to appropriate salvation we must respond to God's offer by taking the necessary steps:
  o We must hear the gospel message (Rom. 10:14).
  o We must believe what we hear and obey it. The scripture calls this faith (Jas. 2:17).
  o We must repent of our sins (worldly lifestyle) and live for God (Acts 26:20).
  o We must combine our faith and repentance with confession that Jesus Christ is our Lord (Rom. 10:9).
  o We must be baptized (immersed) for the remission of our sins and reception of the Holy Spirit (Acts 2:38).
  o We must live the Christian life (1 Peter 1:13-15).

All these steps are essential in appropriating God's offer of salvation. It is our belief that since the first century church preached this message of salvation, the twenty-first century church should do the same. Like the Anabaptists, we do not accept infant baptism as a valid salvation experience. Neither do we accept a Sinner's Prayer as an acceptable response to the gospel message. Salvation by any other means than what

---

[206] William A. Gerrard III, <u>Walter Scott American Frontier Evangelist,</u> (College Press, 1992), 123.
[207] Ibid., 149.

the New Testament teaches is a man-made invention and subverts the plan of God.

Conclusion

I am delighted that some religious groups who have espoused the Sinner's Prayer for years are reevaluating their practice in light of the Scripture. It is refreshing to know that Christian people are willing to change their beliefs and long standing traditions in order to follow a biblical pattern. Our hope and prayer is that all churches would be willing to take such bold steps. God's gracious plan of salvation should be embraced and shared with the world. It should in no way be changed or manipulated for the sake of winning converts.

Conversions In the Books of Acts

Those Converted	Preaching Hear	Believed	Repented	Confessed	Baptized	Salvation
Pentecost 2:14-47	2:14-40		2:38		2:38, 41	2:38, 47
Samaria 8:5-13	8:5-6, 12	8:12			8:12-13	
Eunuch 8:26-39	8:35	8:36-3?		8:37	8:38	8:39
Saul 9:3-19; 22:6-21	9:6; 22:12-16				22:16	22:16
Cornelius 10:1-11:18	10:33; 11:14				10:48	11:14, 18
Lydia 16:13-15	16:14				16:15	
Jailer 16:25-34	16:32	16:34			16:33	16:30, 34
Corinth 18:1-11	18:4, 9, 11	18:8			18:8	
Other Scriptures	Rom. 10:17; John 6:44-45	Heb. 11:6; John 8:24	Luke 13:3; Acts 17:30-31	Rom. 10:9-10; Matt. 10:32-33	Gal. 3:26-27; 1 Pet. 3:20-21	Mark 16:16;Heb. 5:8-9

This chart (or similar versions) has been published for several years in many different publications. I do not know who originated it so I cannot give the proper recognition.

Brooks Genealogical History[208]

BY
Lawrence Sonley

---

[208] Lawrence Sonley, <u>BROOKS GENEALOGY OF A FAMILY OF THAT NAME</u>,(October 1983), N.P.: www.melissacravenfowler.com/Genealogy.html. Internet. (Retrieved May 3, 2016). Used with permission.

INTRODUCTION

During the research process of my book I discovered a reference to Elisha's diary. Louise Davenport, author of <u>Academia On The Pine</u>, said she talked with Alice Brooks Dowland, a niece of Elisha, and was able to obtain notes and excerpts from Elisha's diary. I became determined to find this diary if possible.

Much to my consternation, I learned that Louise and Alice had passed away many years ago. I was able to contact some of Alice's family but unfortunately, no one knew of the diary or where it may have ended up. Upon searching the internet, I came across a document written by Lawrence Sonley about the Brooks family. Much to my delight, I read how Mr. Sonley had met with Mrs. Dowland and read from the diary also.

I was hopeful in trying to contact Mr. Sonley since the document listed his address at St. Louis, Michigan. I was able to contact family members of Mr. Sonley but was told that he had also passed away several years ago. Since Mr. Sonley had no immediate family living, I was given permission by Melissa Fowler, relative of Mr. Sonley and owner of his publication to reprint some of the pages from his document.

Lawrence Sonley is a great-great-great-great nephew of Laura Brooks, Elisha's wife. It was his intent to write a history for the Brooks family focusing specifically upon Elisha and Laura's genealogical line. The document is seventy-five pages in length and gives historical information about the family plus genealogical lines of Elisha, Laura, and Elisha's brother Othniel.

What I have reprinted on the following pages is the historical information about Elisha, Laura, and Othniel since it includes direct quotes from Elisha's diary. I have printed the information as it was exactly written by Mr. Sonley. At this point in time, I believe that this is as close to Elisha's diary that I may get.

ELISHA BROOKS

The composition and precise handwriting of his diary give evidence that Elisha was a literate man, despite the fact that his schooling did not extend beyond what was locally available during his boyhood in the small community of Braceville, Ohio.

Obliged by circumstances to live with aged and probably stern grandparents, understandably his childhood was grim, and dishearten : So, not surprisingly, by the time he reached self-supporting age, he was filled with ambitious dreams of independence, wanderlust and adventure. He left home at 17.

An excerpt from the diary, written near Vicksburg, Mississippi when he was 23, reveals the traumatic effect which his parents' untimely death had on him and his siblings. Also, the entry provides a brief account of his early travels. In his own words:

> ". . . Of that once happy family consisting of eight persons, one half were soon laid low in the tomb and four unhappy orphans were left to wander their unhappy way through a cold and heartless world.
>
> "My eldest sister has since married Daniel Jacobs, and now resides in Lima, Allen County, Ohio; my second sister married Joseph L. Frary and resides in Windham, Portage County, Ohio; my brother Othniel was living in Braceville, Trumbull County when I received the last information from home.
>
> "I lived several years in the neighborhood where I was born, but left there the 18th of October, 1835 and went to Lima, Ohio, where I lived until the 10th of October, 1838, when I repaired to Cincinnati, then descended the Ohio River and the Mississippi as far as the mouth of the Arkansas; I remained there until October, 1839 and descended to the Island One Hundred and remained there until September 1840, then descended to the Yazoo River, where I now remain this date, March 22nc, 1841.
>
> "As I have received no communication from my friends lately, I suppose they do not know where I am at this time, and as I an in a land of strangers and far from my friends, I have written these few lines from a sense

of duty to ny relatives, so that in case some unforeseen accident should befall me, I hope that this book may fall into the hands of some friend who will send it and my trunk to: Daniel Jacobs, Lima, Allen County, Ohio."

At that moment, youthful ambitions seem to have palled; there was a hint of despair--a general disillusionment with life. (Perhaps the dark mood of that particular spring day was due to fatigue or illness.)

Within a couple of years, more or less, Elisha worked his wax-back north, presumably returning to Ohio for a visit. Then, still footloose and looking for new horizons, he headed for Indiana, It is not now known how or when he became acquainted with the family of Otis and Zipporah (Coats) Bartlett, formerly of Gustavus, Ohio (twenty-odd miles northeast of Braceville). However, in Newville Township, DeKalb County, Indiana — April, 1845—he married Laura Bartlett. He was 27 and she 15. By 1848 they had two sons.

Discovery of gold in California, offering the prospect of quick riches, was a temptation Elisha could not resist. Leaving his wife and children with his in-laws, in 1849 he joined a westbound wagon train—which survived acute shortages of food and water on separate occasions. Unsuccessful in his search for gold, after a time he succumbed to discouragement and homesickness. Dreading to make the rigorous trip back to Indiana via the overland route, he took a boat to the Isthmus of Panama, then shuttled across the Gulf of Mexico and up the Mississippi and Ohio Rivers.

No date is recorded, but sometime between 1850 and 1854, Daniel, the eldest child, died.

When news was learned that government land in parts of mid-Lower Michigan was available at a bargain price, in September of 1854 the 3-member Brooks family packed their possessions and travelled by team and wagon to Maple Rapids in Clinton County. Settled in 1835, that frontier trading post was at a junction of Chippewa Indian trails which crisscrossed the center of the state.

A mile and a half northwest of the hamlet, Elisha left his wife and son at the home of Arnold Payne, the first permanent white family of the county named Gratiot. (Having located near the county's southern boundary in 1846, the Paynes welcomed whomever wanted to stop over.)

Going onward alone, twenty-five miles northeastward in Gratiot County, he reached the settlement of Pine River (named St. Louis in 1865), which had been founded by a half dozen families during 1853 and '54. Scouting the area for suitable farm land, four miles beyond Pine River he selected 160 gently sloped acres or. the north edge of the county (NWk of section 1, of what became Pine River Twp. the following year) . To transact the $80 purchase, he chen had to backtrack fifty miles southwest to Ionia, where the Government Land Office was located. The conveyance was made Oct. 10, 1854.

Prior to August, 1854, the price of government tracts had been $1.25 per acre, available to anyone 21 years of age or head of a family. But, because a lot of prairie land was accessible in other states and territories, few people were attracted to the forested wilds of Michigan. So, to encourage rapid settlement there, a Congressional act reduced the price to fifty cents an acre. Each purchaser was permitted to have 320 acres, but after enactment of the new price it was foreseen that some investors might undertake improvement of the land at their individual leisure, thus delaying development of the area. Conseqently, a retroactive order required every fifty-cents-an-acre buyer to occupy his property within one year from date of purchase, or forfeit his land and payment.

Until white inhabitants arrived, the area was a nearly impenetrable wilderness of trees and undergrowth; but in 1853 the founders of Pine River village had widened a narrow, meandering Indian trail into a wagon road, thus creating an arterial transit route between Pine River and Maple Rapids. Afterward, travelers who sometimes found a segment of the road impassable simply hewed themselves a detour.

The Indian population of the county was not large, and members were peaceful, accepting the intrusion of white men without resistance. For quite some time a small tribe of Chippewas had lived by the Maple River near the southern edge of the county. In 1S48 the Lutheran Church established a 1200-acre mission along the west side of the Pine River a couple of miles inside the county's north boundary. That school/church, known as the Bethany Mission (and Indian town), also served as a trading post. (The Indian footpath between Maple Rapids and the Mission was what the founders of Pine River village had followed when they first entered the area in 1853.) As white men's diseases decimated the Maple River natives, remnants of the tribe went to the Mission. In 1856 the federal government granted the state's scattered tribes of Chippewas a reservation in Isabella County, and by 1858-59 the Indians of Gratiot moved there. Timewise, therefore, the ten-year period of biracial coexistence in the county was less than is commonly supposed today, and much less than was experienced in other regions of the nation, both before then and after.

The first priority of every settler was construction of a shelter. Until the first sawmills made lumber available in 1856, dwellings had to be built of logs.

Returning from Ionia, Elisha stopped at the Paynes to see his wife, then went on alone to their place at the top of the county. The first day, he put up a bark-sided shanty as temporary cover for himself, with an open fire pit for cooking his meals. With team and tools, in the following days he got a house started before snowfall began in early November. Chinks between the logs were stuffed Inside and out with wet clay, which heat from the fireplace then baked hard. Roof shakes (shingles), consisting of wood slices three feet long and an inch thick, were made by driving a rive (a special 16" x 3" blade) through pine blocks with a maul.

Toward winter's end he was anxious to bring his family from the Payne place before spring rains turned the road into quagmire. But because the winter was long, with snows lingering into April, the wagon could not be used; so he contrived a makeshift pung (crude sleigh) to which he hitched the team and made the trip.

With lodging built, each farmer then quickly cleared away enough brush and stumps so a small crop of grain and vegetables could be grown. The first year or two, only food for family could be produced-- little for sale or barter. Horses and cows subsisted mainly on wild forage.

Before the county's first grist mill was built at Elyton (Alma) in 1857, the nearest mill where flour and corn meal could be ground was at Muir in Ionia Co., a distance of forty-five miles. A round trip to Muir took at least four days.

Due to the swampy flatlands eastward from Pine River village, access to Saginaw in summer was a flatboat ride on the Pine and Tittabawassee Rivers. Foating downstream took a day and a half, but return trips were three to four times longer, because supply-laden boats had to be portaged around shallow portions of the wincing Pine. The overland route to Saginaw could be traversed only in winter when the terrain was frozen.

With livelihood established, farmers then concentrated on the backbreaking job of clearing more land--removing the wilderness to make way for further crop production. Until that was accomplished, dependence on small, acreage resulted in a narrow margin of survival when adverse weather diminished harvests, as was the case from 1856 through 1859.

The only thing that prevented wholesale starvation was an abundance of wild game and emergency provisions donated by sympathetic down State citizens. Settlers with little foresight--no experience or cash reserves--were totally unprepared for the challenges of frontier life. From the poverty of those years, the county gained a reputation of being a wretched place in which to live. Some people gave up and left, but despite the rugged existence most of the pioneers adapted and endured.

Sales of government tracts at 1854's reduced price caused a land rush, and the imminence of sudden population growth in the county raised the need for local government. An act of the state legislature in February 1855 authorized the formation of townships and the first election of officers. Being public spirited and able, as were many of the pioneers, Elisha ran for office early on. In 1856 he served as Treasurer of Pine River Township, and Justice of the Peace in 1857.

Surprising as it now seems, a post office was established at Pine River as early as the fall of 1855. To facilitate the flew of mail in the rural area north of the village, Elisha was appointed to operate a branch at his residence (Feb. 24, 1857 to June 17, 1859). For the purpose cf giving the office its own address identity, it was called Forest Hill, a description of Elisha's hilltop homestead. Thereafter, the branch office passed to the homes of other postmasters until it came to rest at a small settlement five miles southwest of where it started. That is how the present village of Forest Hill got its name.

After lumber became locally available for construction, about 185S or '59 Elisha built a frame house, and the log hut was abandoned.

From the day Elisha left his grandparents' care in 1835, unti he settled in Michigan twenty years later, his means of livelihood involved assorted forms of hard physical labor. In Michigan, farm ing was his main occupation, but he also was a dedicated purveyor pulpit religion. Sometime during the course of his early life a r ligious bent began asserting itself; also, his father-in-law, a Un ed Brethren preacher, undoubtedly was influential. A passage in t book "Churches of Christ" (of Michigan) reveals that he had been a member of the Disciples of Christ denomination in Indiana. Whethe he ever received any formal instruction or ordination from a schoo of religion is not known, but by midlife he was recognized as a su cessful "evangelist."

About 1861 an evangelist from Indiana visited central Michiga With Elisha's collaboration, revival meetings were held at Pine Ri er and Salt River (Shepherd, in Isabella Co.) villages. The forma tion of several small churches resulted.

Before church buildings could be afforded, meetings were held at schoolhouses or residences. Membership of the Forest Hill congregation quickly outgrew its quarters, so three branches were fori ed: one remaining there, one at Pine River and one at Pleasant Rid (Coe, in Isabella Co.). Living near Pleasant Ridge, it was conven lent for the Brooks family to attend services there. After a few years, they transferred their membership to St. Louis (formerly Pi River).

Soon after arriving in 1855, settlers made plans for educatin their children. The first school in Pine River village was erecte in 185 7. (By 1867 the county had 61 log and 24 frame schoolhouses An exact date is not known, but approximately in the late 1860s or early '70s Elisha thought St. Louis was ready for a facility more advanced than elementary grades. Under his promotion, and the support of local Disciples of Christ, a small stock company construct an imposing frame building atop the hill on the north edge of the river; and Elisha was the first president of The St. Louis Academy Association.

Although there is no precise record of its duration, the venture was short-lived, abandoned before 1879--as public inte est in a private school was insufficient to support its continuanc During the late 19th and early 20th centuries the building success fully served as Yerington's College, where commercial courses and music were taught. After that, the structure stood vacant a numbs-of years until razed in 1952.

★★★★★★★★★★★★★★★★★★★★★★★★★★★★★★★★★★

Born over a period of twenty-eight years (1845-1873), Elisha and Laura Brooks had eight children. The following biographical briefs describe the lives of the four who survived to adulthood.

★★★★★★★★★

Born in Indiana, son Daniel, as already noted, died there.

★★★★★★★★★

Warren, the second child born in Indiana, married Emaline, daughter of Amos and Eleanor (Reeves) Payne of Greene Co., Pennsylvania. As farmers, they lived their years together on the south half of the acreage which Warren's father had homesteaded. There, they raised three daughters and a son: Angelina, Alta, Elsie and Bliss. Another daughter, Mintie, died at age 8. Emaline died in 1915. Sometime in the 1920s Warren moved to a farm two miles south, where he remained until his death in 1933.

★★★★★★★★★

In Michigan, daughter Jessie was the only one of the children born in the log house before it was replaced. She married Charles Dutt, one of thirteen children born to (?) and Lydia (Hoover/Ruber) Dute. (Some of the children changed the spelling of the name to Dutt.). The Dutes were of German extraction and lived in Venango Co. Pa. Charles could not speak English until he was nine years old, when he taught himself to read and write. Later, some of the Dutt offspring, and their widowed mother, settled in central Michigan or. farms near Riverdale (Gratiot Co.) and Vestaburg (Montcalm Co.). Elizabeth, one of Charles' younger sisters, was the mother of Conrad Riess, the husband of Warren Brooks' daughter Angeline. Jessie and Charles were farmers in Coe Township, Isabella Co. (section 26), where they had three sons and a daughter: Meade, Clyde, Ruth and Charles. About 1908 they moved to Alma, Mich, where Charles engaged in carpentry. In 1916 Jessie and Charles went to Tulsa, Oklahoma where he continued to ply his carpentry trade. A couple of years after Jessie died there in 1921, Charles went to

Los Angeles, California where he lived with his eldest son, Meade, until Meade's death in 1930, after which he resided at a retirement home in San Gabriel, Calif.

★★★★★★★★

California, Lincoln and Laura, the fourth, fifth and sixth offspring respectively, died in childhood.

★★★★★★★★

Flora, the seventh child, married Chester Alexander who was born in Lenawee Co., Mich, to Mortimer and Mary Alexander. He was a telegrapher until age 21. Married to Etta Baker at Holt, Mich, in 1883, they moved to Isabella Co. where two daughters, Bessie and Dora, were born. Etta died in 1892, and the following year "Chat" married Flora Brooks. They lived on his farm (Coe Twp., section 27) until the early 1900s when they went to St. Louis where he was affiliated with a meat market. After 1909 they returned to the farm and built a new barn in 1915. Around 1920-21 they lived in Shepherd two or three years while Chet worked for a livestock shipping co-op. Back on the farm again, when Chet's health declined in the '20s, they moved to a house at the east edge of the nearby settlement of Coe, keeping their farm for rental income. Nine miles east, along the Pine River in Porter Twp., Midland Co., they owned 112 acres of summer cow-pasture. Directly after Chet died in 1932, oil was discovered in that part of Porter Twp. With income from oil wells, Flora was able to have a winter home near Tampa, Florida; also, she funded construction of a dormitory at the summer campground of mid-state units of the Christian Church at Rock Lake in Montcalm Co. Flora had no children of her own. and both stepdaughters preceded her in death.

★★★★★★★

The eighth and youngest child, Nellie, wed Anson Fowler, one of four children born to Edward and Eunice (Eddy) Fowler. In mid-Michigan the elder Fowlers were farmers, but prior to their establishment there both Edward and Eunice had been school teachers in Hillsdale Co., Mich. (Earlier forebears — Fowler and Eddy--had roots in New York state.) Anson was born on the south boundary of Isabella Co., adjacent to the Elisha Brooks farm on the north side of Gratiot Co. Thus Nellie and Anson were next-ccor neighbors. Married, they were farmers and lived on the north half of what had been Elisha's homestead. After Elisha died in 1891, his widow, Laura, lived with Nellie and Anson the remainder of her years. The Fowlers had one son and one daughter: 0. S. and Ketha. About 1935, or soon after, they began going to Florida with Nellie's sister Flora, their winter home being nearby at Dunedin.They wintered there every year until 1958.

OTHNIEL BROOKS

At age 13, Othnlel left his grandparents' home in 1835, the same year his brother left.

Employed in the lumbering trade and other occupations for twelve years, by 1847 he had enough savings to buy a 72-acre farm near Braceville, Ohio.

At nearby Warren, Ohio, in December of the previous year, he had married Lois Wilmst, daughter of Randall and Mary (Grant) Wilraot. Randall was born in Woodbridge, Conn, and Mary in Sullivan Co., N. Y. Lois, born at Bethany, Pa. (Wayne Co.), had a half brother, David Wilraot, who became a Pennsylvania congressman in 1844. Sometime between 1832 and 1843 the Wilmots moved from Pennsylvania to Braceville where they owned a general store.

Othniel sold his first farm and that marked the beginning of involvement in real estate ventures for nearly three decades in Ohio, wherein a series of farms were bought and sold for profit.

Of five children born to Lois and Othniel, daughter Jessie was the only one who survived. Lois died in 1865, at age 40, and four years later Othniel married Mercy (Tucker) Russell, daughter of Charles and Tamar (Middleditch) Tucker. Mercy was the widow of Dr. Robert Russell, M. D. A number of Tucker families lived in eastern Trumbull County at that time, Emily Tucker, one of Mercy's sisters, married Collins Bacon whose family founded the settlement of Bacons-burg, now known as Cortland (9 miles northeast of Warren, 0.).

Othniel and Mercy had three children: daughter Nellie died at age two; sons Fred and Gale survived.

Alone, early in 1875, Othniel went to Gratiot Co., Mich, where his sister and brother lived. From one landholder, on March 8 he bought five separate farms — totalling 235 acres—at a cost of $4,000. He returned to Ohio and, in the fall, after the birth of son Gale in September, moved his family to St. Louis, Michigan.

By that time, twenty years after its founding, Gratiot Co. had a population of more than 12,000 and boasted many marks of progress.

As farmers and logging crews cleared away the forest, the lumber industry fluorished. In addition to a number of local sawmills, Saginaw also received some of the flood of trees being cut. Every spring, at high-water time, great drives of pine logs were floated to downstream mills.

The three principle communities of the county, St. Louis, Alma and Ithaca, were boom towns of commerce. Several hotels, a couple of newspapers and two banks symbolized the tide of prosperity. Completion of a plank road between St. Louis and Saginaw in 1869, and a railroad in 1872, accelerated the shipment of wood products from the area. With those transportation improvements at hand, several cooperages (barrel factories) were a big business while the timber lasted.

Assuming that this unit of the Brooks family availed itself of railway service to mid-Michigan, the journey from Ohio was made in relative comfort--in contrast to the rugged wagon and foot travel which the first settlers had withstood twenty years earlier.

Just beyond the northwest edge of st. Louis, the family took up residence on a 75-acre portion of the original multi-farm purchase. The hilltop hone had a sweeping view of the river and village below. (Prior to their ownership, the existing house had served as a boarding house for men employed in local Industries.). From age 54 until failing health forced his retirement in the 1890s, Othniel farmed and conducted a sideline real estate business, as he had done in Ohio.

When he died in 1896, Mercy returned him to Braceville, Ohio for burial beside his first wife and deceased children. She continued living on the farm at St, Louis. (On some records, her name is spelled "Mercie".)

★★★★★★★★★★★★★★★★★★★★★★★★★★★★★★★★★★★

At the time of its publication in 1884, a book of Gratiot Count biographies stated that Jessie, the surviving daughter of Othniel's first marriage, was living; however, Othniel's grandchildren today-know nothing of her fate. The family has no record, either written or oral, of her ever having lived in Michigan. When Othniel, Mercy and the two boys moved to Michigan in 1875, Jessie would have been 15 years old; and possibly she married and remained in Ohio.

★★★★★★★★★

From the time of Othniel's health decline until well after his death, his elder son, Fred, worked the family farm--a period of mere than a decade. In 1895 Fred married Jessie Hinkle and they had two sons, Jay and Francis, the first of whom died within a year. Around 1905 or '06, he and his family went to Detroit where he was employed as a conductor for the interurban railway. There, son Francis died, at age 13, of accidental gunshot wounds received while playing with a boyhood friend. Jessie died in 1918 and Fred remarried.

★★★★★★★★★

Son Gale learned the baking trade at Ithaca and then, with a partner, opened a bakery and restaurant in St. Louis. In 1902 he married Pearl Caldwell, daughter of Seldon and Alice (Sprague) Caldwell. Their first home was on Delaware St. in town, two or three blocks south of Washington Ave. (near where the city water tower new stands). In 1906, after Gale's brother went to Detroit, they moved to the home farm, which he operated the rest of his life. There, with the help of his carpenter father-in-law, extensive improvements were made during the course of the next several years.

Electricity, central heating, a cistern, running water and hardwood floors were installed in the house; and a woodshed was replaced by an attached garage. In the farmyard, a tool shed, two-story granary and silo were added.

Local electricity had been produced in St. Louis since 1883, by a water-powered generator at the town's dam site. Used first for street lighting, it was extended to commercial and residential buildings by the turn of the century. Telephone service also became available. By 1909, downtown business streets were not yet paved, but board sidewalks were being replaced with concrete. Rows of horizontal "hitching posts" for horses still lined the streets, although use of wooden posts had given way to steel piping. Automobiles made their appearance and, within a couple of years, began to be commonplace.

Of seven children born to Gale and Pearl, two died in infancy. The survivors were: Alice, Grace, Lena, Gale Jr., Doris. Pearl died in 1918 and in 1920 Gale married Ava (Bond) VanBenschoten Sprague. (Ava's second husband had been Thurman Sprague, one of Pearl's first cousins.) In the mid-1930s, during the oil boom in nearby Midland County's Porter Township, the upstairs portion of the big house was converted into two apartments which were rented to oil workers. Gale lived until 1952 and Ava until 1971.

★★★★★★★★★★★★★★★★★★★★★★★★★★★★★★

Despite a goodly rate of propagation throughout the Brooks generations, the number of male members perpetuating the family surname has been relatively small. That meagerness is consistent among the descendants of Elisha and Othniel, wherein there exists today only one family unit from whom the Brooks name has any chance of continuance. That prospect rests with the offspring of Gale Brooks' son, Gale Jr.

★★★★★★★★★★★★★★★★★★★★★★★★★★★★★★

LAURA BARTLETT BROOKS

The name Bartlett is of English origin and literally means descendant of little Bart, Bart being a nickname for any man named Bartholomew,

★★★★★★★★

The 1850 census of Newville Twp., DeKalb Co., Indiana, gives Otis Bartlett's birthplace as Canada. It is surmised that his parents moved there from New England after the Revolutionary War. His marriage to Zipporah Coats was probably about 1827. They are known to have resided in Trumbull Co., Ohio, for a time, inasmuch as the census lists their first three children as having been born there.

A history of DeKalb County, published in 1859, reveals that the first permanent white settlers of Newville and Stafford Townships located there about 1836. The author of that book stated that "Within a few years afterward, quite a number moved in," Among thoe named as having been among the "afterward" arrivals was Otis Bartlett. Correlating that fact with Harmon Bartlett's 1845 birth in Pennsylvania and Laura Bartlett's April, 1845, marriage to Elisha Brooks in DeKalb Co. pinpoints the family's time of migration to Indiana as late winter or early spring of 1845. It is assumed that other Bartlett families in the area at the time were relatives of Otis. Coats families also there may have been Zipporah's kin.

Indiana residency of the family was not long. On September 6, 1857, in Gratiot County, Michigan, Otis bought (from an individual, not the government) forty acres on section eleven of Pine River Township (SW 1/4 of the SE 1/4).

The 1850 census lists Otis' trade as "cabinet maker," Although resources of the farm contributed to the family livelihood, it was his skill as a furniture maker and carpenter that was the main means of support. His interests, however, were not confined solely to worldly work, he also was a self-styled preacher. The book <u>History of Gratiot County, Michigan</u> (1913) accords him the title Reverend and states that he was "a well known expounder of the gospel." The author of that book, having been personally acquainted with him, added that the man was "somewhat crude and eccentric, but esteemed," Elisha Brooks' son, Warren, once remarked to his niece, Ruth Dutt Estes, that his grandfather Bartlett had been a "United Brethren preacher, but rather mixed up in his beliefs."

The cause of Otis' death, at age 92, is officially recorded as "old age." No tombstone marks the site, but he and his wife are believed to be buried at the west-central edge of the Coe (Pleasant Ridge) cemetery in southeastern Isabella County, near the unmarked burial plot of Warren Brooks' daughter Alta and her husband, Thomas Leonard.

Zipporah, the unusual given name of Otis' wife, was of Biblical origin (Zipporah was the wife of Moses) . Oral history perpetuates a claim that Zipporah Coats was related to the Coats family once prominent in the sewing thread industry. No effort has been made to substantiate that claim.

★★★★★★★★★★★★★★★★★★★★★★★★★★★★★★★★

Charity Bartlett, at age 15, married Leverett Totten. Deed records show that the Tottens purchased forty acres from the government on Nov. 17, 1855, on section one of Pine River Twp., Gratiot Co., Mich., (NE 1/4 of the NE 1/4)--the same section on which Elisha and Laura (Bartlett) Brooks homesteaded. Leverett also was a blacksmith and was the first smith in Pine River (St. Louis). His shop was near where the city water tower now stands. Charity and Leverett lived only sixteen years after settling in Michigan--both dying in their forties. Of their six children, three produced offspring, but the family tree resulting from those three now numbers more than 1,400 members.

★★★★★★★★

Laura Bartlett, as the wife of Elisha Brooks, shared most cf her husband's life story, as recounted in the biographical text of this book.

★★★★★★★★

Maria Bartlett (pronounced ma-RYE-a) was a school teacher by the age of twenty, as documented in the following letter written by Warren Brooks to The St. Louis Leader about 1926 or '29.

> When reading of so many school activities in different localities, I thought perhaps a few items in regard to the early history of the Elm Grove school district would be of interest to at least a few of your many readers.
>
> The first school in this district was taught by Maria Barclect, in 1857, in a little log cabin owned but unoccupied by old Uncle Sylvanus Sias on what is now known as Curtiss' Corners. One night during the term, the building caught fire and burned down, supposedly

from an overheated stove. This proved quite a serious loss as the scholars lost practically all their school bocks, the supply being somewhat limited at best. However, the term was concluded one-half mile west in a little log cabin owned but unoccupied by Watson P. Reed, on what is now known as Kiter's farm. If not the first, this was one of the first schools taught in Pine River Township.

The following season the district erected a hewed log structure on the original site. It was 16 x 24 and composed entire ly of pine logs. The seats, desks, chinks and shingles were hand shaved. Even the door steps were two large pine logs flattened on each side, and extended the full length of the front end of the building.

Following are the names of the scholars who attended this school: Charles and Sarah Robinson, Will and Dan Vanderbeek; Will, Mioma and Ellen Holmes; George, Deborah and Mira Mecum; Mitchell, George and Villa Packer; Harmon and Judson Bartlett; Genalia Groom, Frank and Ann Henerett, and Marion Caldwell; Henry and Laura Totten, and Warren Brooks. Of all this happy, rollicking bunch of school children, only three remain: Laura Totten Davison, Villa Packer and Warren Brooks.

Maria never married. At Saginaw, sometime in the 1860s or '70s, terminal cancer was diagnosed, and she died on the way home --buried near the roadside at a location now unknown.

★★★★★★★★★

Nothing is known of the fate of Roswell Bartlett.

★★★★★★★★★

Harmon Bartlett bought a residential lot in St. Louis in May, 1867. He married Elizabeth Dexter the following year, and in August,

1869, sold the St. Louis lot to his sister, Laura Brooks. Where he lived thereafter and whether he had children is not known.

★★★★★★★★★

Judson, the youngest Bartlett child, familiarly called "Jud-die," had a colorful career in the ministry. At the age of nine he joined the United Brethren Church, then transferred to the Church of Christ (Disciples) when he was fifteen. About 1884 he and his wife went to Vestaburg, Montcalm County, when it was still a lumbering village. While centered there the rest of his life, he preached for varying lengths of time at eight churches scattered throughout that county--all of which were at small, country sites that have nearly disappeared from today's maps. He had no children.

NOTES

The author is not a member of the Brooks bloodline. His interest in the family stems from the fact that he is a great-great-great-nephew of Elisha's wife, Laura. He is descended from Laura's sister, Charity, who married Leverett Totten in 1844. Thus, all descendants of Laura (Bartlett) Brooks and Charity (Bartlett) Totten are cousins.

At first, the idea for this book was to have a roster of Laura's descendants (and a separate book of Charity's descendants) for the purpose of preserving knowledge of the Brooks-Totten relationship. That idea changed, however, with the telling of Elisha Brooks' ancestry.

Also, it was appropriate for the story of Elisha's brother, Qthniel, to be told. This book, in a sense, closely unites descendants of the two brothers, recording knowledge of their cousinship before it is lost.

(Note: Charity Totten's descendants are related only to Elisha's segment of the Brooks family tree, not to his ancestors or to Othniel 's branch.)

APPENDIX E
Randal and Letitia Faurot Pioneer Educators[209]

Randal and Letitia Faurot were pioneers in their own right. They started several Disciples congregations in Ohio and Indiana. Little did they know that their ministry at Newville, Indiana would have a huge impact upon Restoration Movement advancements in Michigan. We do not know when Randal met and baptized Elisha Brooks, however, within a few years after that event the Faurots would move to central Michigan and become ministry partners with Brooks and Elias Sias.

In spite of their evangelistic successes, the Faurot's passion was in education. They are foremost noted in Restoration annals for starting academies wherever they went. The information on the following pages was written about them while living in Newville.

Randal Faurot, A. M., was born in the town of Hopewell, near Canandaigua, N. Y., in 1820. He was the seventh son of Randal and Urana (Dolittle) Faurot, who moved to Royalton, near Cleveland, Ohio, when he was twelve years of age. Hav-ing a desire for an education, he relinquished his share in the prospective fine farms for a few terms in an academy and the time to study. As soon as competent he taught school in the winter and devoted his summers to study, and finally entered Oberlin College where he remained several terms. He subsequently graduated from Bethany College, Virginia.

In early life he took a decided stand with the Disciples of Christ and worked earnestly with the people who built up so many large churches

---

[209] Biographical information was obtained from the <u>History of DeKalb County Indiana,</u> (Chicago: Inter-State Publishing Co., 1885), 707-709.

of devoted Christians on the Western Reserve, Ohio, and soon became a successful preacher as well as teacher. While on a visit to his father and brothers who had moved to Michigan, he met the natural orator and revivalist, Benjamin Alton, whose labors were so productive of good in Ohio, Michigan and Indiana, and engaged in holding meetings with him in Stafford, Newville, Coburn's Corners, and other points. Feeling drawn toward this part of the vineyard, he decided to remain in De Kalb County and became of great assistance in building the churches at Newville, Waterloo, Kendallville, Mishawaka, Edgerton, riding on horseback over the rough roads, and in addition to holding meetings, visiting the sick and afflicted, comforting the poor and needy, and leading many to righteousness.

He was largely instrumental in the building of Newville Academy, which flourished and was a great source of good for many years. Newville Church of Christ history gives 1854 as the beginning of the Academy.[210] His memory is held in grateful remembrance by many in different states, because of his arduous labors in the cause of education.

He was a persistent and thorough worker. His work was never left half done. He was strongly opposed to secret societies, and was a clear, shrewd debater, carrying his audience with him more by the force of his logic than by his persuasive powers. Kind and thoughtful, his greatest desire was to be useful to his friends, finding his greatest pleasure in seeing those he loved happy.

While preaching in Philadelphia, he wrote and had published, "Pilgrim's Progress," a book written in imitation of John Bunyan, in which he showed the advantages and joy of living a Christian life. It was a work of great interest to a Christian, and of benefit to a young convert, and he received many letters, acknowledging the help derived from its perusal, and thanking him for giving the public a work of the kind.

At the breaking out of the Rebellion[211] many of his students enlisted, and it was the wish of some that he should go as their Chaplain, but one

---

[210] Daniel Farrer, History of the Newville Church of Christ 1851-1991, (Newville, Indiana, 1991), 2.

[211] The Rebellion was another name given to the American Civil War. James Joyner, "The War of the Rebellion and the Naming of the American Civil War, " Outside the Beltway, (August 20, 2013). Www.outsidethebeltway.com. Internet, retrieved May 3, 2016.

who knew him well, said : "No ; Elder Faurot could not look on sin and intrigue with sufficient allowance to work among those who so misused each other." However, he and his wife went twice to Tennessee during the war, first as volunteer nurses after the battle of Murfreesboro, and again to look after wounded friends.

While there they lent such valuable aid in starting schools for the colored people that he was subsequently called South to locate a school for the oppressed race, and after many months of labor, during which he was engaged much of the time in missionary work, he, with Dr. W. A. Belding, located the Southern Christian Institute on an old plantation of 800 acres, lying on the railroad fourteen miles east of Vicksburg and twenty-six miles west of Jackson, Miss. Here in the midst of the work he builded, and which was as dear to him as his own family, he died Oct. 10, 1882, the day before his sixty-second birthday.

Newville Academy. IMAGE COURTESY OF WILLIAM H. WILLENNAR GENEALOGY CENTER, A SERVICE OF ECKHART PUBLIC LIBRARY.

He was married in May, 1847, to. Letitia Hutchings, in Cortland County, N. Y. She had preceded him in the pioneer educational work of De Kalb County, and there they met in 1845. She proved a worthy help-meet for a noble man, sympathizing with him in all his work, and aiding him by her counsel and prayers in all his varied vicissitudes. Her kindly ministrations to the sick and oppressed endeared her to the hearts of all who knew her. They had no children to gladden their home, but reared from childhood a motherless nephew and niece, Marvin Faurot Hall, of Hillsdale, Mich., where he attended college, and subsequently located and is engaged in the electric-light business; and Mary L. Hutchings, now the wife of Dr. W. P. Andrews, proprietor of the magnetic springs at St. Louis, Mich.

Their home was ever the home of the widow and orphan, and the weary and oppressed were ever welcome, and given a resting place. Truly, the deeds of the good live after them and shine as bright stars in the crown of their rejoicing.

Newville Academy was originally called Vienna Academy after the township. When Randal Faurot became superintendent, the name was changed to Faurot Academy. In 1856 the name was changed again to Newville Academy and was used as a Township Common School.[212]

---

[212] John Martin Smith, <u>DeKalb County, 1837-1987 Volumes One A and B</u>, (Auburn: DeKalb Sesquicentennial Inc., 1990), 665-666.

Bibliography

"America." Article on-line. Available at http://faculty.washington. edu/qtaylor/a_us_history/0000_1600_timeline.htm. Internet. (Retrieved February 19, 2016.

Billy Graham. Living in God's Love - The New York Crusade. New York: G. P. Putnam's Sons, 2005.

"Billy Graham," Wikipedia. Https://en.wikipedia/Billy_Graham. Internet. (Retrieved October 10, 2014).

"Billy Sunday." Wikipedia. Https://en.wikipedia/Billy_Sunday. Internet. (Retrieved April 3, 2016).

Blodgett, Jan. Protestant Evangelical Literary Culture and Contemporary Society. Connecticut: Greenwood Press, 1954.

Boyd, R. Vernon. A History of The Stone-Campbell Churches in Michigan. Detroit: N.P., 2009.

Brown, John T. Churches of Christ. Louisville: John P. Morton and Company, 1904.

Bunyan, Paul. "Pilgrim's Progress." Wikipedia. Internet. (Retrieved October 10, 2014).

Butler, Burris. "Memories of Early Days in Michigan." Christian Standard. Vol. LXXX No. 39 (September 23, 1944): 6.

Brooks, E. H. "Michigan." Christian Standard. Vol. VIII. No. 15. (April 12, 1873): 119.

Carpenter, L. L. "Brooks." Christian Standard. (November 12, 1890): 17.

Chapman Brothers. Portrait and Biographical Album of Gratiot County. Midland: Chapman Brothers, 1884.

Coombs, J. V. Religious Delusions: A Psychic Study. Cincinnati: Standard Publishing, 1904.

Cottrell, Jack W. "Baptism According to the Reformed Tradition." Baptism and the Remission of Sins. David W. Flecher, editor. College Press, 1990.

Davenport, Louise. ACADEMIA ON THE PINE The Landmark That Was Yerinton's College. Ithaca: The Gratiot County Historical Society, 1981.

Davis, M. M. How the Disciples Began and Grew. "Phillips Bible Institute Series." Cincinnati: Standard Publishing Company, 1915.

Disciples of Christ. District Year Book 1900. Indianapolis: Disciples of Christ, 1900.

_____. District Year Book 1901. Indianapolis: Disciples of Christ, 1901.

_____. District Year Book 1910. Indianapolis: Disciples of Christ, 1910.

Disciples of Christ Historical Society. "Log Home Picture." Nashville: 2003.

Dorsett, Lyle. "Profile In Faith: D.L. Moody." C. S. Lewis Institute.org. Internet. (Retrieved September 10, 2014).

Easton Church History. 125th Anniversary. Easton Church of Christ, 1994.

Errett, Edwin. "Sixty Miles to Be Baptized." Christian Standard. Vol. CXXVII, No. 20. (July 25, 1942): 1-2.

Errett, Russell. "The Muir Semi-centennial." Christian Standard. Vol. XLII, No. 39. (September 29, 1906): 8.

Farrer, Daniel. History of the Newville Church of Christ 1851-1991. Newville: Indiana, 1991.

Faurot, R. "Michigan." Christian Standard. Vol. III No. 30 (May 9, 1868): 149.

_____. "PERSONAL." Christian Standard. Vol. VI No. 33 (August 19, 1871): 267.

Finney, Charles G. Lectures On Revivals Of Religion. New York: Leavitt, Lord & Co., 1835.

"Finney, Charles Grandison." Wikipedia. Internet. (Retrieved December 6, 2014).

Franklin, Benjamin. CHRISTIAN EXPERIENCE SINCERITY SEEKING THE WAY TO HEAVEN. Cincinnati: F. L. Rowe Publishers, 1856.

_____. <u>The American Christian Review</u>. (1856-1878).

Fremont First Christian Church (Disciples of Christ) Centennial (1880-1980): On file with the Disciples of Christ Historical Society: Nashville, Tennessee.

Galli, Mark III. "Revival at Cane Ridge." Christianity Today, Issue 45, 1995. Christianitytoday.com. Internet. (Retrieved November 20, 2014).

Garrett, Leroy. <u>The Stone-Campbell Movement</u>. Joplin: College Press Publishing Company, 1981.

Garrison, J. H. "State Agencies," <u>The Christian</u>. (January 27, 1881).

_____. <u>The Christian Evangelist</u>. (October 30, 1890).

Garrison, Winfred Ernest and Alfred T. DeGroot. <u>The Disciples of Christ A History</u>. St. Louis: The Bethany Press, 1948.

General Missionary Convention, <u>Proceedings Of The General Christian Missionary Convention</u>, October 23-26, (Cincinnati, 1879): 12-13.

Gerrard, William A. <u>Walter Scott American Frontier Evangelist</u>. College Press, 1992.

Girdwood, Robert L. <u>The Restoration Movement In Michigan</u>. N.P.: N.P., 1975.

_____. <u>The Stone-Campbell Movement In Michigan</u>. N.P.: N.P., 2001.

Harris, Sean. "The Sinner's Prayer: Biblical or Extra-Biblical" Http:// pastorseansblog.blogspot.com/2010/07/sinner's-prayer.html (Retrieved November 16, 2014).

Hawes, Gary L. <u>The Life and Times of Isaac Errett</u>. Ph. D. diss., California Graduate School of Theology, 1984.

<u>History of DeKalb County Indiana</u>. Chicago: Inter-State Publishing Co., 1885.

Howard, John R. <u>Christian Banner</u>. (October 11, 1890).

_____. <u>Christian Banner</u>. (November 1923).

"Huguenots." Article on-line. Available at https://en.wikipedia.org/ wiki/Huguenot. Internet. (Retrieved February 3, 2016).

Hurd, J. "DIED." <u>Christian Standard</u>. (August 16, 1873): 261.

"Ionia Yearly Meeting." <u>Christian Standard</u>. (October 23, 1869): 340.

Jackson, Wayne. "The Sinner's Prayer-Is It Biblical?" Christiancourier. com. Internet. (Retrieved November 14, 2014).

Joyner, James. "The War of the Rebellion and the Naming of the American Civil War." Outside the Beltway. (August 20, 2013). Www.outsidethebeltway.com. Internet. Retrieved May 3, 2016.

Kennedy, D. James. Evangelism Explosion. Wheaton: Tyndale House Publishers, 1970.

Klaassen, Walter. Anabaptism in Outline. Herald Press, 1981

Kruger, Frank O. The Origin and Development of the Churches of Christ (Disciples) in Michigan, 1835 to 1930. Thesis, Butler University, 1949.

Leonard, Bill J. A Sense of the Heart. Abingdon Press, 2013.

Lewis, C. S. "Surprised By Joy." Wikipedia. Internet. (Retrieved November 20, 2014).

McAllister, Lester G. & William E. Tucker. Journey in Faith, A History of The Christian Church (Disciples of Christ). St. Louis: The Bethany Press, 1975.

McDowell, Josh. Evidence That Demands A Verdict. Campus Crusade For Christ, 1972.

McIntyre, Patrick. "The History of the Sinner's Prayer, The Graham Formula." You Tube Video.

"Memories of Early Days in Michigan." Christian Standard. (September 23, 1944): 6.

Meese, J. C. "The Restoration Movement in Central Michigan." Christian Standard. Vol. XLIX, No. 29. (July 18, 1914): 1237-1238.

Miano, Tony and Matt Slick. "Is The Sinner's Prayer Biblical?" Christian Apologetics and Research Ministry (CARM). 18 March 2013. Internet.

"Muir Semi-centennial." Christian Standard. (September 29, 1906): 3.

Murch, James Deforest. Christians Only. Cincinnati: Standard Publishing Company, 1961.

Netting, Park H., Velma Morehouse, and Uldene LeRoy. A History of the First Church of Christ. Owosso, Michigan, 2014.

Nettles, Tom. "Billy Sunday, Part 3: Jack Rabbits and Creeds." FOUNDERS. March 24, 2015. Internet. (Retrieved May 23, 2016).

Nevin, John Williamson. The Anxious Bench. Chartersburg: German Reformed Church, 1844.

"Officers of the Sunday-School Association," Decatur Morning Review. August 8, 1884.

Olsen, Ted. "Southern Baptists Debate the Sinner's Prayer." <u>Christianity Today</u>. June 20, 2012. Christianitytoday.com. Internet. (Retrieved September 10, 2014).

"Open Doors, Open Hearts, Open Minds." Cascade Christian Church, Grand Rapids, Michigan. Centennial Issue (1864-1964): 5. On file with the Disciples of Christ Historical Society: Nashville, Tennessee.

Perry, Ellen. <u>100 Years St. Louis Centennial 1853-1953</u>. St. Louis, 1953.

Quidort, Darryl. <u>A History of Coe Church of Christ - Sesquicentennial 1863-2013</u>. (St. Louis, 2013).

Riddle, M. "Correspondence." <u>Christian Standard</u>. Vol. 2. No. 43. (October 11, 1867): 341.

Robinson, John W. <u>A History of Forest Hill Church of Christ 1859-1994</u>. N.P.: N.P., September 25, 1994.

Schaff, Philip. "Baptism." <u>History of the Christian Church; Nicene & Post Nicene Christianity AD 311-600</u>. Vol. III. William B. Eerdmans, 1910.

_____. "Infant Baptism." <u>History of the Christian Church; Ante-Nicene Christianity AD 100-325</u>. Vol. II. William B. Eerdmans, 1910.

Schreiner, Thomas R. and Shawn D. Wright. <u>BELIEVERS BAPTISM SIGN OF THE NEW COVENANT IN CHRIST</u>. Nashville: B&H Publishing Co., 2006.

Severance, Diana. "Billy Sunday Found the Prairie." <u>Christian History Institute</u>. Christianity.com. July 2007. Internet. (Retrieved November 16, 2014).

Sias, Azariah Boody. <u>Sias Family In America 1677 to 1952</u>. Orlando: Florida Press, 1952.

_____. <u>Sias Family In America 1677 to 1952</u>. Vol. III. Supplement 2. Orlando: Florida Press, 1967.

Sias, Elias. "Cascade." <u>Christian Standard</u>. Vol. XIX. No. 13. (March 29, 1884): 102.

_____. "Faurot." <u>Christian Standard</u>. (October 12, 1901): 30.

_____. "MICHIGAN CHRISTIAN MISSIONARY CONVENTION." <u>Christian Standard</u>. Vol. VI No. 33 (August 26, 1871): 269.

_____. "Michigan." <u>Christian Standard</u>. (February 27, 1886): 70.

_____. "Union City." <u>Christian Standard</u>. (May 6, 1871).

"Sinner's Prayer." <u>Wikipedia</u>. Internet. (Retrieved November 3, 2014).

Smith, John Martin. <u>DeKalb County, 1837-1987 Volumes One A and B</u>. Auburn: DeKalb Sesquicentennial Inc., 1990.

Sonley, Lawrence. <u>BROOKS GENEALOGY OF A FAMILY OF THAT NAME</u>. October 1983, N.P.: www.melissacravenfowler.com/Genealogy.html. Internet. (Retrieved May 3, 2016).

Staten, Steven Francis. <u>The Sinner's Prayer</u>. Interactive Bible.com. 12-03-2007. Internet. (Retrieved August 10, 2014).

"Stroke." <u>Christian Standard</u>. (October 14, 1893).

Sullivan, Roderick Beebe Jr. "Rev. Eleazar Wheelock." <u>Wheelockgenealogy.com</u>. Internet. (Retrieved November 19, 2014).

"The Church by the Side of the Road." <u>History Of The Ferris Church of Christ</u>. (August 22, 2003): 2.

"Theology of Anabaptism." <u>Wikipedia</u>. Internet. (Retrieved September 12, 2014).

Torrey, R. A. <u>How To Bring Men To Christ</u>. Fleming Revell Co., 1893.

"Transactions of the Grand Lodge." <u>Transactions of the Grand Lodge - Free and Accepted Masons of the State of Michigan, A.D. 1888 - A.L. 5888</u>. St. Louis: Masonic Grand Lodge, 1888.

Tucker, Willard D. "Pine River Township." <u>History of Gratiot County</u>. Saginaw: Seeman & Peters Press, 1913. On file with the Historical Society of Gratiot County. Ithaca, Michigan.

Watts, Joel L. "Easy Believism." <u>Unsettledchristianity.com</u>. Internet. (Retrieved November 19, 2014).

Webb, John. <u>Christ's Suit to the Sinner</u>. N.P. N.P.

West, Earl Irvin. <u>The Search For The Ancient Order Vol. I A History of The Restoration Movement 1849-1906</u>. Nashville: Gospel Advocate Company, 1974.

Wise, Keith J. "St. Louis Church of Christ." <u>Centennial Anniversary 1858-1958</u>. St. Louis, 1998.

Printed in the United States
By Bookmasters